T0157928

We Power Us

We Power Us

Green Jobs | Big Oil Subsidies | American Politics

MITCH BOUCHER PE, LEED AP

WESTBOW
PRESS
A DIVISION OF THOMAS NELSON
& ZONDERVAN

WestBow Press books may be ordered through booksellers or by contacting:

WestBow Press
A Division of Thomas Nelson & Zondervan
1663 Liberty Drive
Bloomington, IN 47403
www.westbowpress.com
1 (866) 928-1240

ISBN: 978-1-4908-1784-2 (sc)
ISBN: 978-1-4908-1785-9 (hc)
ISBN: 978-1-4908-1783-5 (e)

Library of Congress Control Number: 2013921428

Printed in the United States of America.

WestBow Press rev. date: 01/13/2014

To my son and daughter,
for their future.

CONTENTS

PREFACE

I have written this book because I think that people need to be informed in order to make good energy decisions to direct local, state, and federal government. It is difficult to stay informed on political issues. It is even more difficult to stay informed on a technical topic like energy and how it interacts with something as double-sided as politics. Yet it is imperative that people stay informed and connected.

Several things have changed over a long period of time, and each makes staying informed more difficult. The changes also contribute to greater disconnection from policymakers and, furthermore, divide us from each other. People used to sit on their front porches and talk to each other as they walked around their neighborhoods. As time and transportation abilities have progressed, people have drifted apart. We may often live and work great distances apart. We are more distant from our families and more distant from our co-workers. We go to work, then we come home, and they are two different worlds. Seldom do we live close to our co-workers. Seldom do we live in areas where we walk around and talk to our neighbors. Those things would be fine in one sense, except that they have not been replaced by a quality communication substitute.

Men would get together during break times and lunch during their daily work and discuss issues. Old men sat in corner cafés and discussed culture and politics in light of the past. Women would talk with each other as they worked out their daily lives, taking care of the home and children, or more recently as a part of the workforce. Today, politics are a shunned topic outside of the home. People are afraid to discuss things that are controversial. That makes it difficult to share ideas and move forward through discourse.

Another thing that drives us apart is the current nature of work. We once had more monolithic work communities. We farmed, or worked in manufacturing, or in some developmental or supportive role to agriculture or industry. That shared work experince gave people common goals. Today, there are thousands of industries and literally thousands of career skills necessary to support the economy. We need people to make our cars, trucks, trains and airplanes, and make them work well. We need to build houses, steel buildings, bridges and roads. We need people to program computers, phones, TVs, and cars. The plethora of available careers has created very different lives and experiences for each of us, thus making it that much more difficult to find common ground.

Meanwhile, the government has shifted from an ideology whereby politicians serve Americans by protecting our basic liberties, which allow people succeed through individual efforts, to an ideology whereby expanded government services are considered rights. That shift has led to inaction and a thorough disconnect with the citizens that the American government is meant to serve.

In the original role, the concept of liberty provides the framework, the opportunity, the freedom for everyone equally to be all they care to be. In its more recent role, US government representatives and senators work, esentially to sell specific services directly to specific groups of people. In order to practice that sort of politics, the politicians must divide us into diverse groups and sell different things like social security, free education, low cost loans, free medical etc., to different groups. This type of governing divides us and focuses us on ourselves. It also results in a big costly government. Compelling people to look inward encourages people to think the government owes them goods and services, exhaserbates the divide in our culture and also destroys the individual drive to succeed.

This book is aimed at two audiences. On the one hand, I hope to present several alternative ideas to those who wish to regulate energy. Those folks who seek to regulate energy seem to pursue their purpose with a somewhat singular idea—that less energy means less environmental damage. However, when energy production is approached with innovation that is enigmatic of a small unregulated business, solutions that surpass regulation *can* be achieved (without expanding government). The other audience I hope to reach are those who want smaller government and the personal freedom to solve thier own energy supply problems, but they lack the informational tools to argue their points. The goal of this book is to inform and subsequently expand the national conversation on energy, to encourage people to then take the message further into their own circle of friends to change the conversation.

People should have the freedom to make energy choices that align with their personal world view. In order for that to happen, we need to free the energy industry from the type of regulation that has evolved from 1970s era legislation. Certainly some regulations are required to maintain a general framework that ensures overall safety (where applicable). Nevertheless, we have been plagued since the 1970s with the idea that we must have a national energy policy to regulate specifically how people and businesses use energy. In government and as a nation, we have struggled to promote an energy industry that honors our personal choices. Creating a free market is an alternative to a "National Energy Policy." It is important because a free market will increase innovation and choices, which ultimately lead to better solutions.

The goal is not re-regulation or de-regulation per se. The goal is to understand that energy as a resource belongs to everyone, like dirt, air or water. Energy is used every day and in so many different ways, that we don't realize that what we choose from the myriad of energy options each day, is in fact a personal choice. Someone who wants to protect the environment should be free to make an energy choice for his or her own use. Those who are on a fixed budget and want low-cost energy should be free to make a choice that will cost less. Ultimately, regulation needs to promote individual energy choices throughout our daily lives, as part of our inalienable rights.

INTRODUCTION

Our Energy Future at a Crossroads

There are two paths which we can pursue in regard to energy. Depending upon which path we choose, we will either become energy rich—or energy poor.

One path is less structured and contains less detail about the government's role. It will be difficult to chart where the path will lead because an abundance of solutions will come from many individuals, and the individual solutions will be weaved together, each built upon the last. It will produce many options, and some of them will fail. People that lose investments in the failed plans will do so by their own free will. They will invest because of the great drive in the human spirit to explore and achieve. The plans that fail will fail "small" and in small numbers because bad ideas will not attract investors.

The less structured plan will also produce many ideas that will succeed. People will invest in ways that have personal meaning for their own individual lives. Maybe a business owner who grew up on a windy plain is driven to develop wind turbines. Maybe a young boy who helped his father in a plumbing business will develop the new pump that enables deep earth high temperature pumping from oil shale fields. Those people that work in those businesses will take great satisfaction in their efforts. Some jobs will pay average wages, some jobs will pay more. Some people will become wealthy due to the millions of uses for their idea. Those ideas will reduce the cost of energy. They will have to produce services and goods at a lower cost than the marketplace in order to succeed. Economic efficiency will increase because people will have more money to spend on other things like their children's education, or a new car to go back and forth to work, or a second car so mom can run errands during the day. Some ideas will reduce emissions and pollution. Overall, The quantity and quality of successful solutions, the cost of services, and energy efficiency will all improve because each idea builds and improves upon the last, and because many people are all working at the same time in so many diverse and different directions.

We will look back at the way things used to be, and be able to tell future generations that the unchartable path provided the best solution. Uncharted paths encourage us to trust the God-given creativity of people and their ability to produce great ideas.

The second plan flows from an overall national energy policy which identifies the most likely successful energy courses. It is structured and developed by a select group of energy experts. The policy is based on an energy model developed with several scenarios of future energy supply, to ensure that multiple alternate courses of action are considered. Government commissions and departments will be created and industry experts will be commissioned to develop implementation plans.

Central planning and research and development costs a lot of money. Some of the projects will fail. They will fail tremendously, because the plan will concentrate large sums of taxpayer money into development until the failure of those projects is undeniable. It will all be funded with taxpayer money, borrowed from future generations of children who will have to pay it back. Because the large-scale failures will destroy large amounts of capital and effort, the economy will be adversely affected. Energy costs will rise, and jobs will be lost. But the government will change their plans and continue their efforts because of the great drive in the human spirit to explore and achieve. They'll also work hard because the rest of society is depending upon them. Everyone looks to the government for a solution.

New regulations will seek to reduce exposure to risks by limiting actions and activities. There will be ozone action days to reduce gasoline use on particularly hot days. Some groups will propose taxes on energy to reduce energy use, because energy supplies will appear to reach crisis levels. Some projects will succeed and produce energy from new sources. Energy costs will rise because development is subsidized and not optimized. Costs will rise because we focused on a particular clean energy, and it was not the least expensive energy. (But we would never know that, because too few of the other options were attempted.)

Since politicians are focused on successes in order to get re-elected, we will only hear news about the good ideas. The good news will lift our spirits. There are still a modest number of jobs available, because the government continues to subsidize energy projects. The taxes to pay for the subsidies are levied on the higher wage earners and small businesses, since they are successful and earn more income. A prosperous solution to the energy supply crisis is never discovered, because prosperity was not the goal. Prosperity is shunned by some politicians in order to create envy, and divide people into special interest groups.

The second plan for our energy future is rooted in the concentration of power and capital at the top, within government. Ultimately, with this plan, few people will end up owning their own businesses. The plan is marked by values that are developed by whoever is in power. This plan does not require individual effort or achievement, since there is no real personal responsibility. It gives people and more importantly government the ability to blame someone or something else for failure.

Which course you believe in depends upon your current experience and your belief in how we came to be on this planet. We will, as a nation, either become energy rich or energy poor as a result of our choices.

CHAPTER 1

Energy

E nergy is a common thread that runs through nearly every part of
our lives. Almost all of us use it every day. We depend upon it,
yet we don't much consider where it comes from or how we get it.
It is there affecting our businesses and our government. It affects us
personally and internationally. Energy provides a level of civilization,
allowing us to use a refrigerator, a phone, or a car. It can be thought
of as a convenience, like having a garage door opener or a TV
remote. But it is really much more than that.

Let's think about the old days.

In the time prior to steam engines and autos, prior to oil and
energy production, people had to produce their own energy for
conveniences. Bathwater was warmed once per week over a wood
fire. The people in the house bathed in order, down to the baby, who
was usually last. Hence where we get the phrase, "Don't throw the
baby out with the bath water." People lived hard lives and cut wood,
farmed the land, and hunted for food daily. Modern conveniences
took the form of tools like a sharp ax or an iron. The iron was literally

a big chunk of iron shaped like our modern day iron. That iron was then set upon the wood stove and heated till hot. It was picked up with a hot pad and used to "iron out the wrinkles" in our Sunday best clothes. Imagine having to plan when to iron your clothes around when the fire was burning. We spent much of our lives doing work that was required just to take care of day-to-day tasks that we now take for granted.

We invented windmill and waterwheel technology, and wind and water powered our tools and inventions to provide convenience and leverage. Windmills and waterwheels helped us to do more work, and made that work easier. We put the turning motion of the wind blades to work. When the wind blew, the windmills would pump water for us. We developed the waterwheel, and towns sprang up around the rivers and waterfalls.

Most of those windmills and waterwheels have disappeared because their necessary resources could not meet everyone's needs (The wind doesn't always blow, and rivers are not portable.) Both inventions were only suitable for a specific purpose, and were limited by their location.

Heat energy is another basic need, and how we use and distribute heat as a resource has changed over the course of history. Early Americans burned wood for heat. The Hopi Indians burned coal in the 1300s. It was rediscovered for heat in America in the late 1600s.[1] Later, James Watt and some others invented the steam engine, around 1770[1]. The steam engine, powered with coal, gave people what they lacked in the waterwheel. The steam engine was a powerful energy source, and it was portable. The steam engine could power trains, and those trains could carry large quantities of goods and fuel across a great distance.

All of these inventions and the energy that powers them have made our lives easier. Before they became part of our lives, making a day-to-day living was defined in the most basic sense. A living back then was defined as eating, sleeping, and keeping warm and dry. In just a short span of years, making a living today now means owning a cell phone, cable TV and having internet access. All those inventions improved upon the one before, and became more efficient. Energy is at the heart of each one.

The point of this little trip down memory lane (other than to give our parents a chance to tell us how thankful we should be) is to avoid current politics and begin a more straightforward conversation about energy sources and their use. There are a few things you need to know about energy and its different forms.

Depending up on your **rate of use**, there is a **storage requirement**. It is **inefficient** to store or transport heat or electric energy, and sunlight cannot be stored at all. Early on, we had to build our towns by the river, and the river needed to have a waterfall. The windmill could not store energy, either.

In relying on water energy, we had to build water towers and water troughs to store the water pumped from a windmill. The energy in the water or wind was not as great as the energy in a lump of coal or in a chunk of wood. The water had to flow for hours to grind a bag of grain. By comparison, a single hopper train car full of coal could power an entire train into the next town. So, energy sources all have an **energy density**. Energy can also be compared by its **thermal** or **mechanical** properties. Water flowing over a wheel, or wind turning a wheel are great for grinding grain and pumping water; coal doesn't fit the bill for either task. But coal and wood are great for burning and heating our homes and heating water to wash clothes. Coal and wood have a great amount of heat (or thermal energy) stored up in their mass. Since the energy in coal, wood, or petroleum fuel is stored as **stable mass**, it is almost 100% efficient to store. Coal and gasoline have a very high energy density, much higher than that stored in wood.

Taking all of these things into account, we can see it is important to match the source energy density and other characteristics to the particular energy use to get the best efficiency.

No one is worried about a terrorist getting on a plane with 3 solar panels. There isn't enough energy produced by the solar panels. If a terrorist gets on a plane with more than 3.7 ounces of gasoline, that's a problem. It is about possessing the right energy to do the right job.

Some people today would have you believe that there are only two types of energy—**renewable** energy and **fossil** fuel energy. Already, you know that energy is much more broad, and that there are more considerations—energy density, storage, efficiency, mass stability, thermal and mechanical, and many other characteristics. They all affect our choices, which affect our standard of living.

When one person mandates that all fuel sources be renewable, that individual is actually ignoring (or he or she may not know) all the technical boundaries of science. Many people espouse renewable energy as though it were the single solution for many geopolitical problems, and it becomes their world view. Fortunately, in the U.S. we are free to follow our own world views. One person can structure his or her life around renewable energy, and another may not. God put all the resources here for us to use, to support us and to sustain us. Because we are free to follow our own world views, the goal should be to develop multiple energy sources and allow people, by free market forces, to make their choices and align the best fuel source to their own individual use.

Now that we've discussed energy sources, let's take a look at an example where proper application of energy sources is crucial.

Alternative Fuel Vehicles

Can you imagine a wood-powered car, or a solar-powered boat? Can you imagine a coal-powered water pump?

We do have solar powered cars. In their current form they are fun solar race experiments for single passengers. Solar race cars take a long time to cross the country. There isn't enough energy density in the solar collector panels to be useful or efficient. It is not possible to pull a train load of corn or steel with a solar-powered train. Solar energy is more efficient as a stationary heating source. It can be made mobile, but only by adding the inefficiencies and complexities of electrical storage.

Solar energy is a low energy density, stationary generation source. By matching the source to the use, it's clear to see that solar is great for buildings. Buildings typically don't move, and they use energy at a slower pace. Therefore, they can use a lower density energy source very well. Furthermore, buildings require thermal energy in the form of heating (for example), which the sun provides.

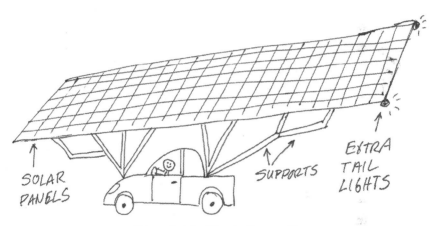

SOLAR PANELS

SUPPORTS

EXTRA TAIL LIGHTS

Figure 1 Solar Electric Concept Car

Now back to the car. A small car is about 100 hp (horsepower). That's about 74,600 watts of energy, or 678 solar panels of the 110 watt type. These panels take up three square feet of space. You have probably seen these in pictures before. They are about two feet high and 20 inches wide. It would take 2,034 square feet of space

Figure 2 Solar Panel Array

in solar panels to give you the same energy density as fuel provides in your current small car. You would have to put a large ranch-sized home full of solar panels on top of that small car to give it the same energy density as a gas- powered car. The car is a prime example of the need to align the energy source characteristics with use characteristics for the best efficiency. Renewable energy has a place and purpose, but it is not a solution for every energy need.

What about hybrid electric vehicles? If you need high energy use in a short period of time, such as acceleration, then you need a high-density energy source like gasoline, natural gas or propane. Hybrid electric vehicles are "hybrid" because they can't store enough electrical energy in the batteries to be truly useful to the mainstream (which is not to say that there is not a use). Electric cars are best intended for a niche market for short around-town personal travel, and not as a long-term viable solution for the transportation sector, because transportation needs are not slow, or stationary.

A top executive at Saphire, an algae fuel research company, put it this way: "…the transportation sector needs an energy-dense, portable fuel. Electric cars are still limited range and expensive, and no one has yet debuted an electric jet."[2]

The source energy density and purpose should match the rate of use and use characteristics in order to create an efficient system by design. Right now, vehicles require a stable, high-density energy source that is lightweight and mobile. Until we develop cold fusion, that source is petroleum, propane or natural gas.

References

1 http://www.fossil.energy.gov/education/energylessons/coal/
   Elem_Coal_Studyguide_draft1.pdf

2 "From Big Oil to Big Algae', pg 89, Fast Company July/Aug 2010, Anya
   Kamenetz

CHAPTER 2

Energy Economics & Green Jobs

When we invented the waterwheel, we introduced a series of economic trade-offs that are still valid today—microeconomic questions comparing how particular work gets done, and the cost and benefit of that work. As we talk about economics, let's introduce a couple of basic economics ideas first:

1. Economic value cannot be created in one area without removing value from another area.

2. There is a synergy made up of labor, capital and energy. They can be substituted for each other to change the economics of an issue.

3. When we increase economic efficiency, we increase economic activity.

4. Increased economic activity creates jobs. Decreased economic activity decreases jobs.

For example, when we work for four hours, with a hand pump pumping a gallon of water, we give up four hours of our life to gain that water. If we pumped enough water for the week, then it may be a good trade off. We give up a part of our life, trading labor to gain something else of value—in this case, water. The economic value of something earned through our work is the fruit of our labor. If we work for four hours each day and then sell the water we have pumped for one silver dollar per gallon of water, then we have created economic value with our labor. This is the essence of the labor equation. Trading labor for other things of value allows us to lift ourselves up and improve our position in life. Economic value cannot be created in one area without removing value from another area. These things are all wrapped up in the labor equation.

In another example, let's substitute capital and energy for labor. Let's say you get an idea to build a windmill and the windmill pumps water. To do this, you can use capital in the form of money to buy the components to build a windmill. You'll buy the blades, the gears, the tower, and then install it over your well. The windmill will pump water longer and faster than you yourself can. You will be able to sell many more gallons of water. Say you decide to sell each gallon for one silver dollar. You have increased economic efficiency. The capital you started with was invested and multiplied by a great idea. You are wringing value out of the wind to produce more water. You can also see here how ideas plus labor create the middle class. It takes all three in some form to make the economic equation work, just like three legs on a stool. The energy from the wind was captured by the windmill, which was built with capital, earned first by our labor.

You could decide to sell the newly pumped water for 50 cents instead of one silver dollar. You can lower water cost to 50 cents because the new system is more efficient. Anytime we can create more output for reduced input, then we will be creating economic efficiency. More people will buy water at 50 cents per gallon. If people only pay 50 cents per gallon today, and it was one dollar per gallon yesterday, then they can spend the other 50 cents on other expenses. That additional spending out of increased efficiency increases economic activity. This increased economic activity employs the maker of the blades, the gears, the tower, the pump, and employs the people who make all the other things people buy with the 50 cents they have left over—even the person who did not build the windmill benefits from the lower cost of water. This is how capital spending creates jobs.

Capital spending alone doesn't create more economic activity, but capital put to work through a more efficient idea creates economic efficiency, which increases economic activity. You can't just spend money. It has to be spent more efficiently. Anytime you can create more output for the same input, then you will have increased your economic efficiency and economic activity.

What about if we work the issue in the other direction? What if we create a rule (or regulation) that we cannot build windmills to pump water? Let's pretend that windmills kill too many birds and windmills are regulated. Let's substitute the labor of two people to pump water instead of using a windmill. Now we get less water for a higher labor input. Our system is less economically efficient. Instead of people paying 50 cents for our water they will have to pay two dollars, and they'll have less money to buy other things. Because of the reduced efficiency, we will have reduced economic activity. If people are not buying other things, then they are not creating any other jobs. However, the scenario did grow more jobs by creating the need to go back to pumping our own water with our own labor.

But did we create jobs by going from capital back to the labor model? No. We had to charge two dollars for the water because we hired additional personnel to pump the water. People bought less overall and paid more for the water, so jobs were lost in other areas. This is an example of job shifting. No new jobs were created. In addition, we have two people working hard to pump the same amount of water. Those people are both poorer. So, instead of one person being rewarded for creating a windmill while the rest of us benefit from low cost water, we are all more uniformly poor.

Simply adding more labor does not create jobs. When we use uneconomic means such as regulations or stimulus to pick and choose jobs and technology, often we are merely cost shifting, or job shifting. It's like taking water out of the deep end of the pool and pouring it into the shallow end to raise the level of the water. It doesn't work.

Energy Efficiency Programs

Do energy efficiency programs like cash for new windows, weather sealing or compact florescent light bulbs create jobs? It is hard to discover answers to complex problems without the right tools or insight. Is there a payback? Is the new system more economically efficient? Yes. In most cases of energy efficiency there is a return on investment.

The very fact that we can invent a way to do the work of heating, cooling, or lighting more efficiently indicates that there is waste in that part of the economy. Inventing a more efficient way to get more output for less input increases energy efficiency. Increasing energy efficiency increases economic efficiency, creates economic activity, and creates jobs.

Energy efficiency is different than energy conservation. Energy conservation plans propose that we do less of something, and therefore get less output with less input. (For example, putting on a sweater and turning down the heat, which is compromising comfort, or using less of something that we desired or needed.) Increasing efficiency is not the same as compromising on the output. Increasing efficiency is inventing a better way to do the same thing with less input. Energy conservation does not create jobs. Energy efficiency creates jobs.

The EPA Energy Star program shows in its 2010 annual report[1] that people who participated in that program saved $20.3 billion in energy that same year. In almost all cases, the people and businesses are still doing the things they need to do, heating, lighting, and cooling their homes and businesses, but with less energy, by their choice. In today's terms, that is $20 billion in economic stimulus that costs zero tax dollars. An energy efficiency project has an average return on investment of about 4 years—a 25% return on investment. The economics of the Energy Star program are much like our water-pumping windmill. People and businesses who invest in energy efficiency get more services for less input. *That* is economic stimulus. Additionally, people are free to choose energy efficiency equipment or ideas according to what works best in their particular situation.

There is also an interesting point here on fair play. When people implement an energy efficiency improvement, the payment for goods and services, and receipt of benefits is completely fair. The folks that buy energy efficiency projects pay capital at a cost agreed upon between the seller and buyer. The payment of capital flows to the innovator and inventor, and the benefits flow back to the buyer. The EPA Energy Star program is a good example of a free market energy efficiency solution. The government burden is small enough that it does not infringe on the free market, and is designed to promote transparency. Information and innovative solutions are developed by the free market, economic activity increases, and jobs are added to the economy.

Renewable Energy Programs

When government programs provide infrastructure at the expense of tax dollars, do they create value? The economy needs roads and bridges and energy to thrive. Let's contrast the economics of the voluntary energy efficiency programs with the federal stimulus of 2010. The American Recovery and Reinvestment Act cost taxpayers over $780 Billion. Those funds were taken from one business and given to another to invest. The businesses and people that paid the taxes did not necessarily get the benefit of the investment. The businesses that paid the taxes and did not take any benefits certainly paid their share, because many paid taxes and received zero benefits.

On the other hand, the money did get invested in some renewable energy businesses, in order to build new capital equipment, like windmills and solar panels. Did those new investments create economic efficiency? No. The renewable energy sources cost more as an input, without an improvement in output. Viable solar PV technologies typically cost 93% *more* than present energy costs.[2] (See more generation costs in Chapter 6.) So we have more input for less output. The energy cost for a clean coal plant is $.11 per kwh. The cost for a baseload PV- generating plant is $.21 per kwh.

Try something—go check your current utility bill, and take the total cost and divide by the kWh usage total to see what you pay now. Now look at the total cost again and double it. That number is what you would pay if we had 100% solar power, and you wouldn't get any additional value, just energy. The economics of the issue are clear if you think of paying twice as much out of your own pocket for the same service.

In the case of the federal stimulus for renewable energy, economic value was destroyed by providing subsidies to more expensive energy technologies to make them attractive. We now know some of the funding went to companies like Solyndra, a company that was not producing viable technology. When a company goes out of business, the investment capital is destroyed, and economic activity decreases.

Energy has a big impact on our daily lives, just like capital, labor and jobs. Energy is used to manufacture almost everything. The cost of energy is embedded first into the raw material and then there's the energy that goes into manufacturing the components of almost everything we use every day. Plastics and many other manufacturing stocks are petroleum-based. If you don't have low-cost plastics and energy, then you don't have low-cost blenders and mixers, cups and plates, plastic chairs, electronics and TVs, computers and phones, shoes and picture frames, cars and bikes, and a whole lot more.

Energy can make our lives easier, or the lack of it can make our lives more expensive and difficult. Renewable energy costs are a tax on the middle class because energy costs are a larger portion of middle class income. When renewable energy advocates say they don't want drilling for petroleum or fossil fuel generation, they are also saying they don't want low cost petroleum-based energy, and timesaving petroleum based products and inventions. That may be a fine decision for their families, but it isn't fair for them to reduce the standard of living for others.

Green Jobs

If you've always wondered what really qualifies as a green job, consider this company recently discussed in *Inc.* Magazine[3]:

A business in New Hampshire drills wells for a living. Their company has now grown to 23 employees. They have about $2.5 million each year in capital equipment and costs. Ten years ago small companies like this could not have made a cost-effective proposal to their customers. However, now that we have improved the technology and availability of parts and pumps, they are growing and hiring.

The technology and quality of high-temperature pumps has improved due to innovation in the private marketplace. (The company received no government funding.)

This company drills geothermal heat pump wells one at a time in people's backyards. The company is not focused on renewable energy; it only uses less energy. It uses electric motors and electricity to "pump" heat from the ground.

Here's a big economic point—Some folks want to raise the cost of energy to make so-called green energy more attractive. If you raise the cost of electricity to produce a better payback on geothermal heat, then you have destroyed the economic benefit of the technology for the customers who buy geothermal heat systems. Higher energy prices mean you will have taken a technology that had the opportunity to use less energy with a lower cost, and you will have changed it to use less energy at the same cost. If there is no increased economic activity, then there is only job shifting and no job creation. The plan by the environmental left to increase the cost of energy to force energy efficiency on the culture more quickly destroys the economic value in the solution and destroys job growth. Any plan to increase energy costs will destroy the middle class' leverage to spend less money and have a better standard of living, improved services, more conveniences, and more value to create a better life.

Used today, the term "green jobs", in truth, implies that people take money from an efficient and productive part of the economy to subsidize work that is less effective and less efficient, and then they charge the customer for the result. Finally, they tax the economy to make up any difference in cost.

Economics, Socialism and Capitalism

Creating value for society over stockholders is the essence of the socialism vs. private business (capitalism) question. Karl Marx complained that privately held capital was not directed efficiently to produce the things that society needed. Therefore, socialism proposed that society shall own all the tools of manufacturing and direct them firsthand. The slogan was, "From each according to his ability, to each according to his need." However, socialism results in a small group of people making decisions for all the others. Someone has to determine who has the ability and who has the need. A small group of people must determine the way capital will be spent and enforce those boundaries by regulations to meet their economic goals. On the other hand, liberty and a free market empower individual effort. But the result of a free market is not distributed evenly among the people. It favors individual effort invested up front. The sovereignty of who makes those decisions is important in our energy discussion because it is the basis for a free markets versus big government discussion. Alexis DeTocqueville interpreted the economic sentiments in America during his visit to the country in 1848, and his writings explain it best. "Each man is the best judge of their own interest."[4] In a free republic or representative government, each person is presumed to be as wise, virtuous and powerful as his neighbor, and therefore capable and free to pursue his or her own work, earn wages and pursue happiness according to his or her opinion. It is important to explore this in more detail because this is the era of big government. Some in government, as well as green energy supporters, believe in a model where they control many of the decisions that drive our economy. Your thoughts on socialism and capitalism will impact your decisions on economics and energy.

Ronald Reagan once said "All systems are capitalist. It's just a matter of who owns and controls the capital – ancient king, dictator, or private individual. We should properly be looking at the contrast between a free market system where individuals have the right to live like kings if they have the ability to earn that right and government control of the market system such as we find today in socialist nations". The first problem with socialism is that "society" could not collectively and separately each own a piece of the factory. Therefore, the state or federal government would own the factories on behalf of the people. Clearly, the socialist premise of capital distribution doesn't really happen, and the wealth never really gets distributed. The people still never direct their own interest or own a piece of the factory.

Another peculiarity in socialism is that socialist or big government advocates like to look at the past and postulate how they would have done it better. Karl Marx looked to the problems of the past and picked some flaws in the economic system of his time. This is similar to how today we can look back at the many stimulus choices that failed. Hindsight is always 20/20 as the saying goes. Nevertheless, those past economic conditions won't happen again, and they will not be the challenge presented by the future. The truth of the matter is that Socialism has no chance of reaching an utopian economy in the future through solving the problems encountered in the past. The solutions for agricultural systems will not work for the modern industrial age. The industrial business solutions from the past will not work for the information age. None of those solutions may work for the energy supply crisis. The economy needs to work in a real-time market of ideas to produce an answer to today's energy supply problems.

Capitalism has its idiosyncrasies too. The overall result of capitalism is that economic efficiency improves. However, it improves in unequal results and unpredictable leaps. The overall result is that society enjoys the improved standard of living. However, most of the economic gain clearly flows to the inventor. Effort and investment are rewarded with results and economic gain—some people get rich. Often this unequal distribution of the end result is seen as unfair or unethical. While it is certainly unequal, it is fair or unfair only after a careful review of the particular ethics of the situation. Ben Franklin said, "The Constitution only gives people the right to pursue happiness. You have to catch it yourself." Abraham Lincoln also believed in rewarding hard work, even if it promoted unequal results.

> *"Property is the fruit of labor...property is desirable...is a positive good in the world. That some should be rich shows that others may become rich, and hence is just encouragement to industry and enterprise. Let not him who is houseless pull down the house of another; but let him labor diligently and build one for himself, thus by example assuring that his own shall be safe from violence when built."*

> —Abraham Lincoln, The Collected Works of Abraham Lincoln edited by Roy P. Basler, Volume VII, "Reply to New York Workingmen's Democratic Republican Association" (March 21, 1864), pp. 259-260

I think most people could look at the number of politicians at all levels that are charged with crimes, and agree that governments are even worse than individuals at crossing ethical lines. The thought that somewhere there is a group of people, first off qualified, and secondly always good intentioned is categorically false. The history of world government is one of tyranny and suffering.

Today, the challenge of wealth distribution can be depicted in a very different light. Karl Marx's proposition was to have the people own the businesses and the tools of manufacturing. Several facts about big business should alter our perception of business and the economy in our century. This new perception should impact our approach to the energy supply crisis. Private ownership of business, whether big, medium or small, is a fair distribution of earnings, and even though sometimes flawed, creates income mobility for the middle class. In the past, businesses were owned and managed by a select few nobles. The limited scale of manufacturing, the physical nature of the work, and the limited access to capital lead to ownership and management by a select few. An individual did not have the right to own property unless he was part of the noble ruling class. Businesses and whole countries were handed down from one generation to the next through bloodlines. Therefore, those old socialists argued that only a few profited in a lucrative way. In that era they were right. Today, in contrast are the employees, the investors, the directors and the beneficiaries of the businesses. We have, in a real measure, achieved the goal of society owning the mechanisms of industry. Big business is not some faceless noble person off in a large building pulling the levers of industry. We are the people who make up big business, first as the workers, then as a middle manager, and finally as the CEO. Business is ever more complex and requires thinkers and managers at every level. and the opportunity to rise from entry level worker to CEO depends mostly on a persons commitment to success. A Gallup Poll[5] in 2011 showed that 87% of Americans who make over $75,000 annually own stock either individually or in an IRA or 401K. We are the ones who benefit when big business succeeds, and we're also the ones who are hurt when big business fails.

Percent of Americans Owning Stocks	
Segment	**Owning stocks**
All Americans	54%
Americans earning over $75,000	87%
All college students	73%
Post graduate students	83%

Figure 3 Who Owns Big Business? (Jacobe)

Government controls will not produce innovation. Capitalism is the mechanism that will produce millions of diverse ideas from each of us regarding how to solve the energy supply crisis—to meet our own interest, to profit individually from our idea—whatever that may be. There is little chance that the government will solve the energy supply crisis, because they cannot find something that they are not looking for. The government is not looking for low-cost and abundant energy. The government is looking for clean or green energy at any cost.

References

1   EnergyStar and Other Climate Protection Partnerships, 2010 Annual
    Report, Table 2.

2   EIA, Energy Information Administration, "Annual Energy Outlook 2011",
    DOE/EIA-383, Table 1, 4/2011

3   Dig Deeper, Bernard Avishai, Inc. Magazine, March 2012

4   Alex DeTocqueville, translated by George Lawrence (1966), *"Democracy in
    America"*, pg 66, (2006) HarperCollins

5   Gallup Poll Social Series: "Economy and Personal Finance", April
    7-11, 2011

CHAPTER 3

A Conversation on Big Government, Big Oil, & Big Environment

There are several sets of forces that shape the conversation on energy. It is almost impossible to have a lucid conversation based in facts unless we unravel some of those forces. Let's look at the public conversation on energy and some other perspectives that impact that conversation. We'll look at how bad choices by big business and big government, both impair the economy and destroy economic freedom. When big governmentand and big business partner with each other, the abuse and waste are multiplied. Furthermore, if it weren't confusing enough, the government also partners with the big environmental lobby to apply pressure in favor of thier partnership. Lastly, we will investigate the "big oil" companies and the stockholders who own those "evil" companies. All these things together influence the energy industry through a political and cultural filter of class envy and social change. Many people don't pause to think and understand why they hold a particular opinion. Strong opinions based on factless ideas develop into conversations that divide people against each other, instead of bringing people together for a common solution. Let's dig into the facts, and explore the different opinions in regard to those facts. We will need to understand these inherent filters as we look forward to energy supply solutions.

Big Government

Big government has grown to the largest size in the history of our country. There are several insidious things that make big government much worse than big business. First, big government never goes away on its own. Politicians never give back power to the people by their own free will. Freedom, once lost, always requires a very tough battle to recover. Big government waste is never punished. Politicians rarely if ever punish themselves to the extent that they hold others accountable. Lastly, big government waste, abuse and fraud cannot exist without big business. So while big government will decry big business, they also require big business to achieve their goal. Think about it, big government cannot make under-the-table deals with 3,000 small business owners. Big government requires and encourages movement of power away from small business and the middle class towards big centrally controlled businesses – which they can tax and control.

The government is big, and getting bigger. *The Washington Post* reported in 2011[1] on the duplication and losses. They cite a Government Accountability Office (GAO) report[2] that states that there are 100 programs dealing with transportation, 82 for teacher quality, 80 for economic development, 47 for job training, 20 for homelessness, 10 complete offices for energy (each with many programs), and the list goes on. There were 292 new legislative bills to deal with energy in 2011 and 2012[3]. That results in an average of 3 new energy laws every week just dealing with energy. The government website FirstGov.gov has a list of all the agencies, each with a department head and staff. It is alphabetized and there are 35 agencies that start with 'a' alone. I did not add up all the letters from a to z.

The GAO issued report idenitified $125.4 billion in improper payments from over 70 different programs in one section alone. That was not the entire summary of savings. There were 80 different recommendations. Did you catch that fact my friend? There were $125.4 billion in savings identified in 1 of 80 different recommendations from the GAO. The government clouds the energy supply crisis conversation by claiming just one more program will solve the energy supply crisis. There are never steps taken to measure if what they have already done has had a positive or negative impact, or if they are being good stewards of the funds they already receive. The incredible volume of legislation leads to complexity and waste.

The best way for us to all come back together, and be less divisive, is to end the system whereby some people get preferential treatment by the government. Over the years preceeding the housing crisis, Fannie Mae and Freddie Mac (the government-private partnership that finances housing) paid $4.8 million in political campaign contributions[4] to politicians. Now, one question is who received that money? It was split near the middle with 57% going to Democrats. The top three recipients were Chris Dodd (D), Barack Obama (D), and John Kerry(D). Before you jump to conclusions, the top six were three Democrats—and the list also included three Republicans. This point is not a left or right political perspective, but a big government point.

Why did Fannie and Freddie give money to politicians? Why does any big business give money to politicians? They do that to get preferential treatment from the government in order to create a monopoly for their product. The partnership of big business and government creates monopolies by perverting the free market to favor their businesses through regulation. Home mortgages are a great example because the government controls over 80% of that market through Fannie Mae and Freddie Mac. Big business wants, and receives special access to people, capital, and to resources through government programs.

Here is the big point—since this chapter is all about big issues. You should recognize that the elements discussed here are the same three inputs to the basic economic equation presented earlier. The basic inputs to the micro economic equation for the economy are labor, capital and energy. So, government-private partnerships clearly distort the free market. Every time a politician proposes another program or partnership, they are adding an impediment to the free market and to economic prosperity. Therefore, the solution to the energy supply crisis is not to add more regulation to distort and force the economic equation in one direction or another. The solution to the energy supply crisis is less regulation and less control.

The biggest business and economic disasters—proof that big government tinkering is never the solution—have all taken place in industries where there is a substantial government-private partnership. These are industries where a government program partners with big businesses and associations like labor unions to take tax money from some people to provide services back to other people. Middle class innovation and small businesses cannot grow and create jobs under the burden of big government regulation. Government-private partnerships benefit big business and big government and destroy economic value and jobs. Think about the government stimulus invested in the banking industry and the management of GM. Both industries continued to suffer huge job losses. General Motors (under the direction of federal government) laid off 75,000 workers between 2008 and 2010[5]. General Motors employees lost about $1.8 Billion from their 401Ks due in part to government receivership of their stock when GM went out of business. The energy industry, which was demonized by the government during the same period for being allegedly evil, was hit equally by the recession, but retained jobs for their employees. Sustainable job growth, where business is successful because of economics, thrives without government involvement. Many banking failures and GM job losses slipped below the media radar.

Company	Total Employees Laid Off (2008 to 4/2010)	
Devon Energy	50	
Chevron	255	
Valero Energy	250	
Hess Corporation	270	
Chesapeake Energy	265	
Baker Hughes	3,000	
Sunoco	750	
Conoco Philips	3,100	
Total	**7,940**	
Ford	4,700	not bailed out
General Motors	75,733	bailed out
Total	**80,433**	
Citigroup	52,175	
JP MorganChase/Bear Stearns	14,000	
Bank of America	35,000	
Balance of Financial/Banks	13,434	
Total	**114,609**	

Figure 4 Job Losses Due to Bailouts (Kneale, Turchioe)

Today a major component of how jobs are created is with an idea and a creative process. Consider that small businesses make up about half the labor force, but create 65% of new jobs. Small businesses also create patents for new ideas at 16 times that of big business. Those jobs all come from an idea coupled with the capital to implement it. The drive to create comes from a very big pool of people who work in small or mid-sized businesses, not in government. They are you and I and your neighbors, working for ourselves and for our companies. Abraham Lincoln said, "Few can be induced to labor exclusively for posterity; and none will do it enthusiastically. Posterity has done nothing for us; and theorize on it as we may, practically we shall do very little for it, unless we are made to think we are at the same time doing something for ourselves."[6]

Even though the things that government folks do is incredibly damaging and sometimes downright unethical, they are people just like you and I, and they make mistakes. The people that make up American government are our neighbors. They have the ability (and when unchecked, the propensity) to do wrong, to make mistakes and to be deceitful. Most of the time, they start out altruistic and truly believe that they are doing good.

Further involvement in the energy industry by government will only lead to the preferential treatment of a handful of solutions. It will not lead to innovation. Further government involvement in the energy industry will lead to more economic and energy disasters. Reducing the size and reach of the government in the energy industry will lead to more innovation from small and mid-size businesses. Innovation happens more quickly when there is more liberty and less regulation. Small businesses can innovate better than big businesses, and big businesses can innovate better than a central government.

Big Oil

We have watched in our time some of the biggest oil and global businesses rise to power and fall to competition or scandal. The success of big business can bring with it graft and crime. There is no doubt that big businesses work very hard to create value for their stockholders. There is also no doubt that in some cases big businesses cross ethical lines. When people who run big businesses are guided by the wrong motives they can cheat, lie and steal. Creating

Company	Lost Capital
Enron	$63 Billion
WorldCom	$103 Billion
MF Global	$41 Billion

Figure 5 Capital Lost by Big Business
(CRS Report for Congress)

value and efficiency for their customer is a part of their job, and is good and desirable when carried out with integrity and honesty. In a free market, customers hold the suppliers accountable to ethical market practices, and fair prices by changing their buying habits. This real-time accountability is the best and most transparent way to regulate commerce. That is my opinion, but the facts will show it to be an honest appraisal of the issue. Even so, the free market is not without error.

Many of us can recall the Enron scandal and what happens when a business is run by unethical people. Enron executives actively concealed transactions and actively deceived the public, government auditors, and their customers. They were convicted and sent to jail. Many will say that it was an error of deregulation, but it was really an example of dishonest executives who lied and cheated their customers and employees.

The government and other groups who oppose fossil fuels use these sorts of issues to rally against big oil businesses. They use the issue to promote their own goals for re-election, and it distorts the conversation of the merits of any particular approach. What went on at Enron was wholly wrong, but it does not mean that fossil fuel as an energy supply is wrong. It also does not mean that green energy as an energy supply is good. So, let's look at some other energy decisions where the benefits cannot be readily measured, and customers lack the ability to change their buying habits.

Government Program	Lost Capital
Fannie Mae, Freddie Mac, Ginnie Mae	$641 billion
Bush(TARP) Bailout	$645 billion
Obama Stimulus	$840 billion
Total Bank Bailouts	$7.77 trillion
Solyndra	$535 million

Figure 6 Capital Lost by Government (NYT, McGuire, Recovery.gov)

Whether a big business fails or a government program fails, capital and jobs are destroyed. Enron was a big problem, but the economic damage grows even larger when the government and big business create a partnership. We demonstrated earlier that legislative programs that take money from taxpayers in one area and give that money to big businesses to hire in another area are not efficient, they destroy capital, and they do not produce any new jobs. This is where the unintended consequence of a national energy policy, in which big business and the government create a partnership, cause really big problems. Let's look at the government and big business partnerships for green energy programs. First, green energy and climate programs are paid for by individuals, but the benefits are proposed to accrue to society. There is no direct connection between the customer and the energy service provider. Secondly, the esoteric benefits of green energy will not be delivered until far into the future, if at all. So many of the people paying the cost will never see the benefit. People can change their buying habits when a business performs poorly.

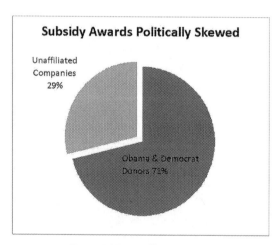

Figure 7 Tax Dollars Used for
Political Favors (Thiessen)

However, government programs never go away, and remove the direct accountability that the free market maintains. In the end, the people who pay taxes will pay for someone elses mistakes, through job loss and a poor economy. But that is not the end of the issue. This is where big business connects back to big government. The politicians in government must advertise their good works to the public to get re-elected. Some politicians take campaign donations in return for political favors to pay for their re-election advertising. The Obama administration steered over 70% of all green energy subsidies to campaign finance committee members or large democratic party donors. So the real problems are covered up by pale shades of truth in barely researched news stories. Both the politician and the business who gets the government grant need the program to be advertised in a good way, and so a scapegoat will be produced to take the blame.

This is the backdrop for businesses in the energy sector of the economy. This simultaneous rivalry and partnership between big business and government serves to create a false narrative in the media. The government wants your vote and is in competition with business for control of your money. The big businesses are in competition with each other for subsidies, and so they strive against each other in the media. The conversation works better for the government if there is a big faceless entity called "big oil." Government works to then turn you against this new faceless enemy, while at the same time earning billions of dollars in campaign donations from the big businesses. In fact, when we look at the ethics of big business, 23% or 3 out of 13 of the Fortune 500 oil and gas companies are on the Forbes "Top 100 Best Companies to Work For" list in 2011[7]. None of the automotive companies made the best companies to work for list, but they made the government bailout list. Big business, big oil and government partnerships distract us from making good energy decisions, and give the government a perpetual excuse for bad policy decisions.

Who Owns Big Oil ?

This is such an interesting point of confusion in energy and business issues. The talking point is that there is some big faceless entity called "big oil" that is the enemy of the middle class. Let's explore this perspective in more detail. First, big oil is really not unlike any other big business. It is a business that happens to work in the industry of extracting a fuel source for our economy. The fact that some environmentalists refer to those businesses as "big oil" makes you wonder if the environmentalist would approve of a "small oil" business. Obviously they would not approve of any oil business. Therefore, we can see that what they have done is create a class envy label in order to rally opinion against those businesses instead of debating the facts. Big business is called big business because a bunch of people work there. It is big business because they do a great job, they develop great ideas, and we keep buying more of what they sell, making them a big business. It is simply the spirit of envy which makes you think that all big businesses are successful by way of ill-gotten gains or by unfair practice. For the energy industry specifically[8], 86% of oil stocks are owned by mutual funds and personal retirement investments. Only 24% of big oil stocks are owned by individuals.

Who Owns Big Oil Stocks?	
Segment	Owning stocks
Pension Funds	31.2%
Mutual Funds	20.6%
IRAs	17.7%
Other Institutional Investors	6.6%
Individuals	21.1%
Oil Company Executives	2.8%

Figure 8 Who Owns Big Oil? (Shapiro, Pham)

Furthermore, only 2.8% of those individual investors are oil company executives. The benefits of business, the 401k dividends and the big oil profits are flowing to society because we the people own the stock of big oil. America owns big oil. We have met the people profiting from big oil and it's us.

Another issue that should change our outlook on big business is one of income mobility. Robin Leach used to host a show on TV called Lifestyles of the Rich and Famous. The show examined the private lives and daily choices and routines of the very rich. Many of those people had very different lives from you and I. But here is the point. At one time, they were just like you and I, and they were striving to provide more for their family. Robin Leach told Fox News in an interview in April, 2012; "We never did a story of people born with a silver spoon in their mouth. And so every one of the people we had on the show was somebody who pulled themselves up by their bootstraps, had worked their tushy off , long hours, long hard work, and they were rewarded by the discipline and diligence and dedication that they applied, with success." So the rich were not always rich, they were people like you and I who developed an idea and worked hard to see it become a success, and they became rich. In fact, about 80% of millionaires are "first generation" rich, which means they started poor and created all their wealth. Some in the media would have you believe that the rich were always rich, and that they are lazy. That is just plain false. That perception is perpetuated with the goal of minimalizing the idea prior to debating the merits of the idea. That false narrative is going to make it difficult to objectively evaluate the source of the best energy supply solutions.

Big Environment

There are several problems for which the big environemental groups are responsible in the energy crisis. First, they use their funding and effort to change the conversation on energy supply development, and they are well funded. Second, the environmental groups focus us on specific issues in the wrong way. The real problem is not so much that we use too much energy, or use the wrong type of energy, but that we have a shortage of innovative and diverse energy sources. If there were other lower- cost, cleaner and more abundant energy supplies, then fossil fuel would become obsolete because there was a better idea. The problem in the interim time is that the DOE and EPA are both aimed at reducing use or limiting access to our natural resources. When the big environmental groups partner with the government, the result is an unstoppable push towards their category of ideas as well as increased regulatory waste, abuse and fraud. Even the DOE efficiency and innovation programs we do have are hampered because they are geared to introduce costly regulations, thereby limiting the actual economic benefit of their work.

The environmental sector seeks to protect the environment by regulating energy as one of their primary purposes. The mission statement of the Environmental Protection Agency (EPA) is: *"Our mission is to protect human health and the environment"* (http://www.epa. gov/aboutepa/). The mission of the Department of Energy (DOE) as stated on their website (http://www.doe.gov/about-us) is: *"The mission of the Department of Energy is to assure America's security and prosperity by addressing its energy, environmental and nuclear challenges through transformative science and technology solutions"*. When you read throught these agencies websites, you learn they are both apparently aimed at reducing pollution from energy sources. They are funded by $37 billion dollars ($27.2B for DOE, $8.9B for the EPA) of tax money each year and the power and force of the Federal Government to reach their goals. If you read through their budgets, their goals are oriented heavily towards compliance. Why is this a problem, you ask? It is a problem because the big environmental groups lobby congress, the same as big business, to gain unequal access to people, capital and resources. Yes, there is a big environmental lobby, you just don't think of them that way. The perception is that big business is organized and well-funded and that the

Big Environmental Funding	
Name	annual spending
Nature Conservancy	$ 1,172,365,000
World Wildlife Fund	$ 151,560,547
Natural Resources Defense Council	$ 119,099,000
Sierra Club Foundation	$ 107,326,908
Environmental Defense Fund	$ 98,100,000
National Wildlife Federation	$ 91,587,821
World Resources Institute	$ 31,658,000
Union of Concerned Scientists	$ 22,000,000
Pew Center on Global Climate Change	$ 11,262,335
Alliance for Climate Protection	$ 88,303,373
TOTAL	$ 1,893,262,984
* 1-10 of 832 other Climate Protection Non-Profit Groups.	

Figure 9 Environmental Groups Spend Big (GuideStar)

environmental groups are all unorganized, mom and pop, live off the land folks, who just want to protect seals and polar bears. The reality is that the environment is big, big business. I went through a handful of the groups that I could think of, and the top 10 are funded annually to almost $2 billion.[9] Additionally, guidestar (www.guidestar.org) had another 832 non-profits just in the climate change category. The big environmental lobby has a great deal of leverage and incredible funding to push the focus of government to their point of view, which is regulation. Big business is also big, but businesses spend only a very small portion of their funding on lobbying. George Soros may well be the biggest business political donor in the world. George Soros' donations were about $550 million over about nine years[10], and much of that was to Universities. When you take into account his $22 billion in net worth, the political lobbying is only about 2.5% in total. The environmental groups focus almost 100% of their funding on their singular goal. The top 10 environmental groups outspend George Soros by 3 times but towards the same goal. They are aggressive, their budget is aimed wholly toward their goal, and they are successful in altering the public conversation to meet their goals.

The Economic Development Administration (EDA) is the only Federal Agency with economic development as it's exclusive mission[11]. The EDA budget is only $300 million in economic development, and even in their agency 5% or $15 million went to a Global Climate Change Mitigation Incentive Fund.

Environmental groups including Greenlaw and the Sierra Club have prevented the construction of 160 proposed coal fired power plants since 2002[12]. Price is a result of supply and demand. This is one reason why our energy prices rise. Additionally, this sort of lobbying to "do nothing" destroys economic activity. I wonder how many jobs those projects would have created? This goes back to that idea that the big environment group is not a bunch of mom and pop groups struggling to make things work for their goal. They are big, well funded and successful.

More recently, government's approach is more about compliance, regulation and central control. That is a different goal than finding abundant or clean energy supplies. Government funding for energy supply research dropped 92% since 1978[13]. Energy supply research was $6 billion in 1978, dropped 92% by 1998 and was about $1.6B in 2008. Today, at $1.6B it is still 75% less than what it was when we were searching for alternate energy supplies in the 1970s. The shift from research to compliance is a direct result of the big environmental groups impacting the public conversation. The almost complete disregard for research and development is amazing. It show the disingenuous nature of the government, when they spend $700 billion on a financial bailout because "failure was imminent," then spend $780 billion on a "stimulus" package, then spend yet another $900 billion on healthcare reform for only 25 million uninsured people. In comparison, they spend less than $2 billion on energy research and development. The environmentalist involvement in the energy supply crisis has not helped the problem. The influence applied to governmnet regulators by big environmental groups dampens innovation because it encourages regulation, not research. The process of finding an enegy supply solution is further hampered when we focus everyone towards the government to look for a handout as opposed to encouraging a diversity of self-funded sources. Therefore, the energy supply crisis is not a natural constraint. There are many energy sources available, but we're not focused on developing them. The current energy supply crisis is caused by constriction of the known natural resources by the EPA and aligned government agencies in response to the demands of the big environmental groups. No other faction or group has as big an advocate in the government as the big environmental groups.

The Truth about Chocolate Cake

One of the things that the big environmental lobby brings to the discussion on energy is an "end justifies the means" approach. The energy supply crisis is a technical and many-faceted problem. It requires a careful review of the facts, and time to gather more data. Many times the environmentalists will compromise on facts to create their version of the truth more quickly if it justifies a new regulation to meet their goal. This makes it very difficult to discuss different options when one group thinks their way is the only right way to deal with such a complex and technical issue.

Here is an anecdote to help you see the balance and thought required for truth. If we were debating the sum of 2 + 2, then there is certainly a right answer. But what is the answer to the question "what is the best chocolate cake recipe"? Now, you see the problem more clearly. There literally may not be a "truth" or a single right answer to the chocolate cake question. Even so, the big environment folks have an intolerance for alternate opinions and an inability to have a discourse on the environmental issues. In *Men's Journal*, Robert Kennedy was interviewed [14] and was asked why we've done next to nothing about global warming. I have a different issue with the "next to nothing" perspective of the interviewer. That is an example of the bias that the media brings to the issue. Nevertheless, Robert Kennedy responded:

> *"One reason* [we've done next to nothing about global warming] *is the irresponsibility of the press. If you've got a press that thinks its job is to tell both sides of the story rather than to tell the truth, then you've got a big problem."*

So you see—the big environment crowd does not even acknowledge other opinions, let alone that the other opinions may be right. The big environment group lacks balance and a real mission that is rooted in the search for the truth. The big environment group is determined to tell you which chocolate cake recipe is the very best, period end of discussion. Given the clear uncertainty in the energy and environment issue, it is unreasonable and unwise to have the government take a lead role in our energy supply industry by aligning with the big environmental group.

Here is another example, some years ago the EPA ordered a natural gas company named Range Resources to clean up the pollution in private drinking wells in Parker County, Texas. The EPA had "determined" that Range Resources was responsible for the pollution, prior to any real investigation. Never mind that there are literally thousands of naturally contaminated water wells all across the US. When you live in natural gas country and drill a well for anything, you can hit natural gas. Sparing you the details, Range Resources did not give in to undue and unfounded government pressure. They were determined to uncover the truth. About 16 months later, the EPA dropped the charges and Range Resources was cleared of all wrong doing. The EPA's role in this example is a different story. Senator James Inhofe performed an investigation, and related some of the details in an inquiry to the EPA. A portion of Senator Inhofe'ss inquiry follows, from one question[15],

> "...Texas State District Judge, Trey Loftin, concluded that one of the residents associated with the EPA's administrative order worked with an environmental activist to create a deceptive video..."

It seems that the homeowner attached his garden hose to a gas relief valve and claimed it was his water hose, then lit the gas coming out of the hose on fire, producing a video that went viral and influenced the public and the EPA. It was a lie. In that same report, Senator Inhofe relates another instance whereby the EPA Administrator for Region VI, Al Armendariz, suggested that the EPA crucify the first company breaking an EPA rule while drilling in the newly discovered gas fields[16].

Administrator Armendariz's response:

> "But as I said, oil and gas is an enforcement priority.... I think it was probably a little crude and maybe not appropriate for the meeting but I'll go ahead and tell you what I said. It was kind of like how the Romans used to conquer little villages in the Mediterranean. They'd go into a little Turkish town somewhere, they'd find the first five guys they saw and they would crudify them. And then you know that town was really easy to manage for the next few years..."

You can't have this sort of abuse of power and enforcement working against the American people in business. It is unconstitutional and a gross misuse of power. It is an example of exactly why the founding fathers refused to give this much power to the government. It was very wise of our constitutional framers to craft laws such that they grant government some specific powers, and all other powers belong to the people. The big environmental groups influence government agencies to create an incredibly dangerous misuse of power. By focusing on the wrong areas with so much intensity, it drains and distracts us from the original goal of finding alternative low-cost and abundant energy supplies.

Summary

All of these forces—big government, big oil, and the big environmental lobby groups shape the conversation on energy. They create a cultural filter and a social conversation that does not produce diverse ideas, because it is their goal to force all thought, funding and regulation towards their one solution. Big business is guilty in this conversation for not taking the initiative to produce alternatives that change the conversation. There is a great market need for clean energy solutions. But we cannot vilify big business too much because big government funding and regulation steered all their work towards solar and wind energy. In the coming years I challenge you to think about the conversations you hear on energy supply alternatives, economics and regulation and see if what you've read here rings true.

Big business is not all evil. It is really just where your friends and neighbors work. Big government is not evil either, nor should it automatically be the solution. St. Clement of Alexandria wrote in a lengthy letter 2,000 years ago, which I will paraphrase for brevity, that "the rich are not inherently evil, and that the poor are not inherently good. But, that each are good or evil depending upon their belief in God, and how that belief directs their life to produce good results." It should not bother us that we will earn a profit, that some people will become well off in their investments and retirement, and that a very few people will become rich.

It is difficult to evaluate any ideas when we are told one of several alternate fables—such as the oil companies are evil, the rich are evil, that anyone who opposes green energy is evil, or that all the free market businesses are run by thieves, and that just one more government program, after 40 years of programs, will solve the energy supply crisis.

References

1   Ed O'Keefe, Government Overlap Costs Taxpayers Billions GOA Reports, March 2011, WWW.Voices.Washingtonpost.com/federal-eye/2011/03/government_overlap_costs_taxpa.html

2   GAO, Government Accountability Office, "Opportunities to Reduce Potential Duplication in Government Programs, Save Tax Dollars, and Enhance Revenue", GAO-11-318SP, March 2011, 205

3   www.GovTrack.us, "Easily track the activities of the United States Congress", http://www.govtrack.us/congress/bills/subjects/energy/6021#congress=112

4   Lindsay Renick Mayer. Fannie and Freddie Invest in Lawmakers, OpenSecrets.org Online, Sept 11, 2008, http://www.opensecrets.org/news/2008/09/update-fannie-mae-and-freddie.html

5   Klaus Kneale, Paolo Turchioe, "Layoff Tracker", Forbes Online, 4/1/2010

6   Abraham Lincoln, speech, 4/22/1842

7   Fortune Magazine, "Fortune 100 Best Companies to Work For", Volume 165, Number 7, May 21, 2012

8   http://whoownsbigoil.org, Sonecon Consulting Study, 2011 Update

9   Guidestar, http://takeaction.guidestar.org/Causes.aspx?cause=Climate%20Change%20%28U.S.%29&ein=13-2654926

10 Dan Gainor, "Soros could just be getting started with $2 million to boost to the left", May 11, 2012, http://www.foxnews.com/opinion/2012/05/11/soros-could-just-be-getting-started-with-2-million-to-boost-to-left/

11 EDA, Economic Development Administration, "Annual Report to Congress, 2022", http://www.eda.gov/pdf/FY2011_EDA_Annual_Report.pdf

12 Barry Cassell, "A Path Forward for Coal", EnergyBiz, March/April 2012, p32

13 GAO, Government Accountability Office, "ADVANCED ENERGY TECHNOLOGIES, Budget Trends and Challenges for DOE's Energy R&D Program", GAO-08-556T, March, 8 2008, http://www.gao.gov/products/GAO-08-556T

14 Jeff Goodell, "Kennedy's Crusade", Men's Journal, June 2012.

15 Senator James Inhofe, US Senate Environmental and Public Works Committee, Letter to EPA Administrator Lisa Jackson, April 25, 2012, http://epw.senate.gov/public/index.cfm%3FFuseAction%3DFiles.View%26FileStore_id%3D7d4b80e5-a4f8-42c0-8c62-8cec8fd5e614Q

16 Ibid

CHAPTER 4

Regulations

"A wise and frugal government which shall restrain men from injuring one another, shall leave them otherwise free to regulate their own pursuits of industry and improvement, and shall not take from the mouth of labor the bread it has earned. This is the sum of good Government."

-Thomas Jefferson

W hat is the role of government in the energy industry? Should government control the natural resources in our country? Should government protect the natural resources? Should government provide equal access to natural resources, for all people and businesses? I have talked a lot about the negative impacts of big central controlled government. Evenso, don't mistake my argument against excessive government regulation for an argument against any form of government. Thomas Jefferson's opening quotation highlights the balance required of good government, and the fact that "good" government is in fact required. We could dissect that quote in great detail and not run out of discussion ideas. There should be government regulation, but it should be done in a way that is wise and careful, and shall be limited in scope and implemented in a frugal way. People generally will always require some regulation to limit injury to one another. However, in other matters such as the economy, industry, and individual pursuits, they should be free from excessive or costly (not frugal) regulation.

So what does good regulation look like? The EPA Energy Star program is one example. It is inexpensive to the taxpayer, and it provides a wealth of information. The final decisions and implementation are left up to the business or individual. Scanner reward laws are another example. In some states in the US and in Canada, if an item at a store scans at the wrong price, the consumer can notify the store and get a reward of $5 or $10 dollars per incorrectly scanned item. The shopper notifies the store, the shopper who was inconvenienced gets the reward, and there is no big regulatory inspection cost to taxpayers. Even though there is no regulatory oversight of the result, the marketplace or shoppers continuously keep the merchant in check. The cost of errors and the ability to impact their regulatory cost is completely with in the control of the merchant.

Government should regulate people's activities when they have a propensity to injure one another, but should otherwise leave people free in their pursuits of life, liberty and happiness. The current level of energy regulation has gone far beyond the role of a limited government, and energy is key to the pursuit of industry and improvement. Because energy is a critical thread that runs through the personal choices of our daily lives, one group cannot make energy decisions for another group of people and still preserve liberty. The environmental lobby believes that the mere use of fossil fuel destroys the environment. Thus, any compromise becomes a discussion from their perspective about how much damage can be tolerated. The compromise from the liberty and free market position becomes one of how much loss of liberty or economic stress can be tolerated before the economy is compromised. It is similar to one group asking the other which finger to cut off. None of the choices is appealing. The difficulty with the regulatory position is that there is no clear natural right for the environmental assumption of the role to protect the environment. People have a right to life, liberty, and the pursuit of happiness. It is an individual right. Our country is a diverse group of people, all with individual ideas, ethics, and morals which flow from worldviews and religious beliefs. The observation during the inception of our country was there are many small groups, and each would insure that no one group would dominate the politic and strip liberty from the other groups. The Federalist Papers describe the purpose of counteracting groups, or the result of those groups as "faction," which means conflict or disagreement. To understand how all this disagreement brings order, we have to again go back to some ideas from the founders of the country.

Whilst all authority in it will be derived from and dependent on the society, the society itself will be broken into so many parts, interests, and classes of citizens, that the rights of individuals, or of the minority, will be in little danger from interested combinations of the majority.

—Federalist Papers #51, 1788, Alexander Hamilton or James Madison

But the most common and durable source of factions has been the various and unequal distribution of property. Those who hold and those who are without property have ever formed distinct interests in society. Those who are creditors, and those who are debtors, fall under a like discrimination. A landed interest, a manufacturing interest, a mercantile interest, a moneyed interest, with many lesser interests, grow up of necessity in civilized nations, and divide them into different classes, actuated by different sentiments and views. The regulation of these various and interfering interests forms the principal task of modern legislation, and involves the spirit of party and faction in the necessary and ordinary operations of the Government.

—Federalist Papers #10, 1787, James Madison

Today, we have strayed far from the original intention of government, which was that we pursue our individual goals in cooperation and at the same time in disagreement with each other. It was understood back then that we would pursue our individual goals with liberty, and we all would not always agree upon things. In fact, continuous unresolved disagreement was key to insuring our individual rights would be maintained. Additionally, people would be the watchdog over the Government, not the other way around. Now we see big government partnering with the environmental groups and at the same time working against free commerce in the energy industry. Regulation aligned with environmentalism are a force restraining commerce. We see liberty and balanced disagreement between factions disintigrate. What group of people is powerful enough to stand up to bold regulation when the government can threaten jail? They have tanks and unmanned airplanes (drones), to enforce their ideas. Regulatory restraint of energy businesses destroys economic value and results in a sluggish economy. Still, some people wonder what the problem with the economy might be.

The environmental groups control many roles of government, and bend regulations to their one interest. The current Energy Policy *Blueprint For a Secure Energy Future*, has only 2-1/2 pages of policies encouraging and enhancing the use of existing domestic energy resources. The purpose of those policies would be to create abundant and low cost energy for the American People. The remaining 35-1/2 pages outline environmental protection regulations, efficiency regulations and green energy research. When one faction proposes to increase the use of our own domestic energy, government regulation acts as a restraining force, encouraged by the big environment group, to enforce that assumed role of protecting the environment. It is important to realize that the disagreement is truly a different opinion in purpose between different factions. The idea that one group is "right" is merely assessing whether or not their opinion squares or differs from your own. The leaders in government need to reframe thier role, which is to provide a balanced and disinterested regulatory backdrop for the pusuit of business.

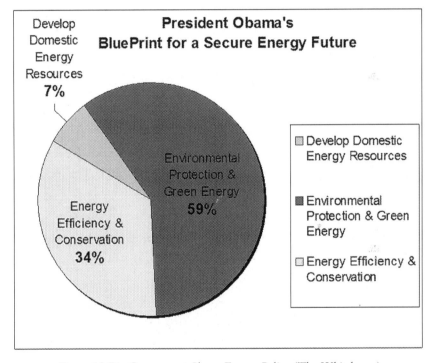

Figure 10 Big Government Skews Energy Policy (The Whitehouse)

The government believes that they have to have regulations in order to protect the people and the environment from abuse at the hands of energy businesses. While this is certainly true in some cases, the founding fathers overwhelmingly believed that it is competition and the freedom of every individual business that will restrain each from injuring one another, and still preserve our individual rights. The cost of goods and services rise in every area controlled by the government. The cost of goods and services drop in most areas when innovation and competition are introduced to the market. So there are truly two opposite approaches to regulating energy. One espouses freedom, liberty and equal access to the nations natural resources in order to innovate our way out of the energy supply crisis. The other approach is to limit access through regulatory practices of central control, and increased costs to make it uneconomic to access our own energy resources. I would propose that we are living the founding fathers' fear that the remedy of regulation is worse than the disease of unfair business practices, especially in the energy industry.

Subsidies

Some in congress have grilled the oil industry on their need for about $4 billion in subsidies. The fact is that the tax code has become a tangled mess of distortions due to government tinkering. Tax incentives are used to "force" people to make decisions that they would not normally pursue, such as buying green energy. Think about it, people avoid a particular course of action because they don't see the value in it for themselves. By forcing one decision over another, the tax code and subsidies distort the natural protections that a free market provides when people each work for their own best interest. Some CBO (Congressional Budget Office) documents clearly state their opinion that the free market does not provide a financial incentive for people to take into account protection of the environment and other "external costs". We can see that idea is an opinion, not fact, by their own further description. This quote highlights in the first and last sentence that tax subsidies are a distortion, and distortions are "good" if the idea aligns with their personal worldview.

> *"Tax policy can be distortionary when firms and individuals change their behavior to avoid paying taxes or to take advantage*

of subsidies. Taxes distort markets to the extent that price signals are altered, leading to too much (or too little) production or consumption. When consumers and producers are more responsive to price changes, price changes resulting from taxes lead to larger market distortions. Not all distortions are bad, as those that correct for externalities, such as taxes on polluting activities, may improve market outcomes."[1]

Subsidies and tax credits are distortionary, period. They force behavior counter to the market cost as the CBO noted. So the tax code as used today overrides the free market and encourages activities that the Government deems "good", instead of what businesses and people think is good. It is not that reducing pollution is not a good idea, it is good. The issue is that some regulations inflate the cost of environmental protection artificially without producing an economic benefit. The regulatory burden or diversion of capital constrains the free market ability to solve the problem through innovation. The result is counterproductive and causes inefficiencies in the economy, causes job loss, and economic destruction. Why would government managers do this? They must truly believe that their idea is better than every one elses. But a central planning government can dilute the entire marketplace of ideas with their own single idea. By contrast, it seems quite easy to see, in the free market model, that all of us working towards many solutions are smarter than one of us working towards one solution. In energy research and development, one government report stated the following:

"The amount of R&D that the private sector undertakes is likely to be inefficiently low from society's perspective because firms cannot easily capture the 'spillover benefits' for society as a whole that result from it".[2]

That comment is ludicrous. In fact, the truth is just the opposite. One only needs to look as far as the Apple© iPad and iPhone products to see the wealth of associated benefits from the free market. The sheer quantity and absolute affordability of cell phones and the availability of 99-cent phone and computer applications for millions and millions of ideas prove the point that the free market is hands down the best innovator for society.

History is the mechanism that brings clarity to the fallacy of central planning through regulation. Subsidies and regulations have grown by huge leaps and bounds over the years and still no utopian age has come. In fact, I would suggest that you can't find two problems that were solved as a result of central planning. I say two, because even a broken clock is right twice a day.

Think of two examples of a social or economic problem government solved (national security and the moon-shot are not included), then ask yourself—Were they first created by some previous regulation? There is an energy supply crisis, a war on poverty, a social security funding crisis, a housing crisis, a financial crisis, an immigration crisis, a political campaign finance crisis, and now a healthcare crisis. The one thing that is common to all of these, is that the government is intimately involved in regulating each. I cannot think of any other area in private enterprise where we have these monumental problems. Where is the scandal when a computer company, lumber, home improvement, appliance, carpeting, lawn mowing, grocery store, bread bakery, soda pop, or mattress company over-charged or cheated us? Where is the cell phone crisis, the car insurance crisis, or the MP3 crisis? There wasn't even a lightbulb crisis until the federal government got involved and outlawed the venerable incandescent lightbulb. You can go into almost any fast food restaurant and get free wi-fi access, and they don't even want to know your name. You can't go into a public library, for which you pay government taxes, and get free wi-fi access that easily. Almost every person in America has electricity, heat and lighting. In February of 1981 *National Geographic* lamented in the preface that we still lacked a national energy policy (National Geographic, "Energy: Facing up to the Problems, Getting Down to Solutions", Feb 1981). Of course we don't have a national computer, national iPad[c], national cell phone policy and we have all the productivity improvements, economic value of those inventions in our lives. The more regulation and policy we have on energy, the less energy we will have. If we do not increase our energy supply, we will become energy poor, or experience energy poverty. We are at a crossroads. We will either return to free market capitalism and innovation to solve our energy supply problems, or we will continue down the road to more regulation.

So in this tangle of subsidies, regulations and tax preferences, where does the money go? Climate change and green energy have received almost twenty times what the oil industry receives. Government regulators complained that the oil industry took advantage of $4 billion in tax subsidies (which the Carter Administration encouraged). The reality is that the government spent $70 billion of your money in total on climate change in the last four years alone[3]. The government easily spent $4 billion on climate change in 1998, and that increased to $7.5 billion in 2009. There was a $39 billion leap in 2010 for stimulus spending[4].

In the last four years the government has spent about $12 billion on tax preference subsidies for fossil fuels, and about $14 billion on tax preference subsidies for renewable energy. The idea that fossil fuels dominate renewables because of subsidies has been categorically untrue for almost 10 years now. Renewable energy is not popular because it is more expensive and less convenient. It's useful to reflect back on the substantial fossil fuel tax subsidies that were put in place by President Carter to "force" more domestic oil production. Then in the late 1980s, it was President Reagan who eliminated oil subsidies because they distort the marketplace of ideas.

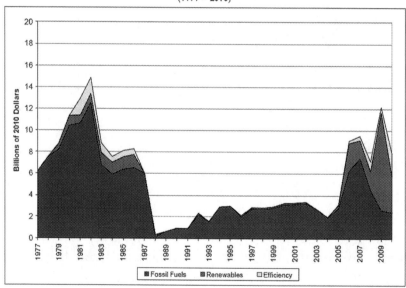

Federal Climate Change Funding, by Category

(Budget authority in billions of 2009 dollars)

Legend:
- International Assistance
- Climate Science
- Technology

Sources: Congressional Budget Office based on Office of Management and Budget, *Federal Climate Change Expenditures: Report to Congress* (various years); and Government Accountability Office, *Climate Change: Federal Reports on Climate Change Funding Should Be Clearer and More Complete*, GAO-05-461 (August 2005), www.gao.gov/new.items/d05461.pdf.

Figure 11 The Government Spent $70 Billion on Climate Change (May)

Tax Expenditures: Incentives for Fossil Fuels, Renewables, and Efficiency
(1977 – 2010)

Legend: Fossil Fuels, Renewables, Efficiency

Source: CRS calculations using JCT tax expenditure estimates and data from the OMB.

Figure 12 Tax Policy Favors Renewable Energy Since 2005 (CRS)

So, the crux of this conversation is how do regulations provide equal access to natural resources, and how does that align with the constitutional role of promoting general welfare? I think direct subsidies are a bad form of encouraging any policy. By their very design, subsidies favor one company or industry over another, which is counter productive to the idea of equal access. I would be in favor of eliminating the big oil subsidies. In addition, all of us are smarter than one of us. This makes the free market a better source of innovation. The risks increase when there is not a diversity of ideas, as provided in the free market. So the government role in promoting the general welfare should mean less controlling and less direct forms of regulation. The list of money wasted by the government by picking winners and losers through subsidies is long and expensive. The renewable energy failures in the last administration alone totaled easily over $7 billion in destroyed capital[5]. When government is too big, there are too many opportunities for money to leak out of the subsidy system as waste. For example, Nevada Geothermal Power got about $98 million in DOE loan guarantees. Then they got an additional $65.7 million in ARRA tax credits[6] under what was called the section 1603 program bringing the total capital destroyed to over $160 million. The total spent on all subsidies through the ARRA section 1603 program on renewable energy was $11.9 billion as of June 8, 2012[7]. The difference between a private company making a mistake and the government making mistakes is that the amount of capital destroyed increases by 10 or 100 fold when a government subsidy is involved.

Capital Destroyed Through Failed Subsidy Spending on Renewable Energy	
Company	Funding (millions)
Raser Technologies	$33.0
ECOtality	$126.2
Nevada Geothermal Power	$98.5
First Solar	$3,000.0
Abound Solar	$400.0
Beacon Power	$43.0
SunPower	$1,200.0
BrightSource	$1,600.0
Solyndra	$535.0
TOTAL	$7,035.7

Figure 13 Failed Government Investments (Thiessen)

Taxes

Of course, you can't have subsidies for renewables or fossil fuels without taxes to pay for the subsidies. In addition to overbearing, one-sided regulations, we are crushed under the weight of the taxation required to perpetuate and enforce regulations. Taxing us to provide the funding to regulate us is like adding insult to injury.

We do need some regulations and some manner of limited government. However, today government "earns" more from the fruit of our labor than the laborer. When you look at a gallon of gasoline, the government earns more from the sale than the oil company and the gas station owner combined.[8] About 23% of the cost of a gallon of gas comes from refining, distribution and marketing.

That 23% includes the profits of the oil companies and gas stations. Their profits range from a high of 28% to a low of 1% and they've averaged 13.8% since 1974. So, the profits of the oil companies are only 13.8% of their 23% chunk of the gas pump, which comes to about 3%. Oil refining distribution and marketing earn about 3% in profit compared to the 11% in taxes that the government takes out of your pocket for a gallon of gas.[9] So gas prices could drop instantly by about 40 cents if the government gave us a tax holiday.

Regular Gasoline (May 2012)
Retail Price: $3.73/ gallon

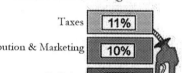

Figure 14 Who Gets Your Gas Money? (EIA)

Furthermore, the 3% that the oil companies make in profits comes back to you and I in the form 401K and IRA account earnings when we invest in oil companies. The 11% taxes are used to fund the big government machine that regulates these businesses, increases costs and drives innovation out of the industry. That capital lost to taxes is essentially overhead, that drives economic efficiency down.

This happens in many other industries as well. According to a *Fortune* magazine article,[10] the airlines pay 14.9% in federal taxes and fees and earn 6.6% in profits. Company profits are paid back to about 54% of us as earnings in our 401Ks and IRAs (see Big Business). The taxes and government fees are essentially overhead and are lost.

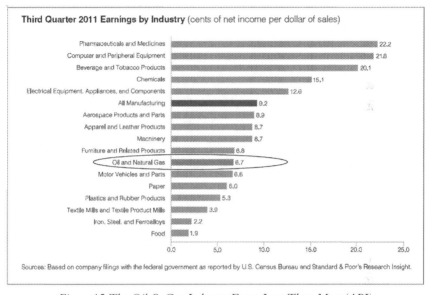

Third Quarter 2011 Earnings by Industry (cents of net income per dollar of sales)

Pharmaceuticals and Medicines	22.2
Computer and Peripheral Equipment	21.8
Beverage and Tobacco Products	20.1
Chemicals	15.1
Electrical Equipment, Appliances, and Components	12.6
All Manufacturing	9.2
Aerospace Products and Parts	8.9
Apparel and Leather Products	8.7
Machinery	8.7
Furniture and Related Products	6.8
Oil and Natural Gas	6.7
Motor Vehicles and Parts	6.6
Paper	6.0
Plastics and Rubber Products	5.3
Textile Mills and Textile Product Mills	3.9
Iron, Steel, and Ferroalloys	2.2
Food	1.9

Sources: Based on company filings with the federal government as reported by U.S. Census Bureau and Standard & Poor's Research Insight.

Figure 15 The Oil & Gas Industry Earns Less Than Most (API)

The government is one of the most lucrative and unregulated big businesses on the planet today. The government has typically taxed us at about 20% as a percent of GDP in the most recent 10 years up to 2008. As of 2011, the overall tax rate (the amount of money the Government keeps) is about 25% of GDP. No other industry earns that much profit.[11] In addition, the taxes are collected unequally among people and businesses. The middle class pays more taxes when energy is taxed, because energy spending takes up a greater part of middle class income.

Subsidies are also paid out unequally and cause an unequal use of revenue and unequal access to natural resources. The Founding Fathers warned of the evils of these types of taxes and duties. Here is an excerpt from Alexander Hamilton from *Federalist Paper #35*, January 5, 1788:

> " *...if the jurisdiction of the national Government, in the article of revenue, should be restricted to particular objects, it would naturally occasion an undue proportion of the public burdens to fall upon those objects. Two evils would spring from this source: the oppression of particular branches of industry; and an unequal distribution of the taxes, as well among the several States as among the citizens of the same State.*"

Clearly the intention of the constitution was not that the government use taxation or regulation to "force" behaviors and preferences towards a particular business. The government is the biggest spender and biggest single overhead expenditure in your life today, period.

Land Leases for Oil and Gas

There is an old folk song by Woody Guthrie that starts out...

> *This land is your land, this land is my land*
> *From California to the New York Island*
> *From the Redwood Forest to the Gulf Stream waters*
> *This land was made for you and me.*

Apparently that is only true if you are the US Government. The US Government is one of the largest land owners in the nation. The oil and gas companies are allowed to drill on a very small percentage of the public land. Even when they drill on land they own privately, they are under very tight environmental controls.

In 2012, the government claimed that they were opening new lands to energy exploration, to encourage our own domestic production. However, the details give a different story. Even under President Bush's first term, you can see the energy exploration on public lands dropping. In President Bush's second term, starting in 2004, exploration dramatically increased from its 20-year decline. Under President Obama, energy exploration dropped (see the figure) sharply to a new 25-year low in 2009 and 2010.[12] The increase in domestic production during the last 3 years is due primarily to the exploration during President Bush's second term, from 2005 to 2007. Once a lease is sold, one to three years is required for the drilling and processing to get the oil and gas to market. New horizontal drilling techniques and improved technology have increased drilling yields. Thus, President Obama taking credit for increased gas and oil production is like the crowing rooster taking credit for the sun rising.

The Bureau of Land Management, which is the government agency responsible for managing the real estate owned by the Federal Government, oversees 700 million acres of land. Most of this land is in about 19 Western states. Those 19 states total about 1.5 billion acres of land, so the government controls about 50% of all the minerals, oil and gas in the West and about 30% of the oil and gas-producing land overall[13] in the country. There are about 27 million acres of protected park and conservation lands, and about 40 million acres leased to oil and gas exploration. Thus you can see that the government has a corner on the real estate market and returns use of only about 10% of that land back to the American people. That is a lot of power and control to be wielded by one agency. The agency has 5 major program priorities. Three of the five programs are conservation-related. Then they have a climate change priority and a new energy frontier, which has renewable energy as its priority. There is no stated goal to develop access to our own domestic oil and gas resources.

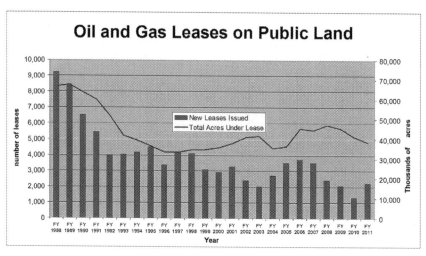

Figure 16 Oil and Gas Leases Drop on Public Land (BLM)

There is a lack of balance and counteracting ideas to represent other groups in the public who want lower-cost energy from domestic resources. One more statistic that may show the impact of this imbalance—while the US Government owns 30% of the land that produces oil and gas, that land only produced about 7.5% of those resources. The other 92.5% of the oil and gas produced domestically is produced from the 70% of privately owned mineral lands.[14] There are more onerous processes and regulatory waste when companies are working on federal lands. Alternately, federal lands could be less rich in resources. Finally, it is worthwhile to point out that the BLM is an executive agency which has a single director as opposed to a board of directors or commissioners to govern their role.

Other Regulatory Costs

Of course taxes are not the only cost of additional regulations. Regulatory costs impact what you and I pay for goods and services. That is especially true of energy since energy is one of the primary inputs to the economy. Ultimately the best case against excessive regulation is that it produces higher energy costs, which in turn depress the economy. In 2011 the government began implementing, by fiat, a regulatory system of cap and trade for mercury and other air toxins. Yes, the "cap and trade" bill was voted down in congress, so the EPA is implementing more rigorous control standards anyway. I know that may be hard to believe, but if you don't believe me go visit the EPA website and search for MACT rules. The cap and trade legislation and increased regulatory controls are another regulatory cost embedded into the cost of energy. Estimates of the cost of cap and trade range from $845 billion by the CBO[15], to has high as $1.9 trillion[16]. This will cost the typical US family about $1,870 per year in additional energy costs. The dollar values in the whole debate varied a great deal, so to bring a little balance and truth to the issue, consider that in Great Britain they are already paying about $1,300 per year for cap and trade rules that have already been in place for a couple years[17]. Thus the cost of cap and trade or other similar regulatory controls is well known. The benefits publicized by the EPA are not measurable or verifiable.

Regulations

In 1975, the Federal Government began regulation to set energy conservation standards for appliances. Since that time, Congress has ceded power to the DOE and EPA to set regulations, thereby forcing businesses to comply with the energy conservation rules through DOE and EPA enforcement. The list of appliances is huge. It impacts every part of our lives, and is now substantially influenced by those agencies. The environmental groups keep pushing for continued intensive work to lower the energy use standard and further testing to insure compliance.

Energy efficiency is great. But there also has to be work on energy supply innovation. This is another example of how big environment groups focus us on the wrong issue too intensely.

The intense desire of the big environment groups to control natural resources, along with their ability to put pressure on the government cause abuses of power. A report by the Lawrence

Berkeley Labs[18] noted that 53% of DOE energy regulations are passed by "rulemaking," and only 47% of the rules are brought before Congress for legislative approval. That means that in their rush to regulate more quickly, they are bypassing due process. In addition, the blind run towards energy use reduction as a primary policy goal causes multiple inefficiencies. As of August of 2012, 6,277 new federal regulations (energy and others) went through in just 90 days![19] Government churns out an average of 70 new regulations each and every day. Do you know what they are? Did you get a chance to vote on the ones that will cost you money? Senator Inhofe reported that by the Federal Government's own estimate, those regulations cost us $1.75 trillion dollars each year.[20] That means it costs each person an average of about $12,000 annually just to pay for regulations.

These regulations are not taxes. They are costs that are embedded into the cost of the appliance, and in the cost of your electric bill. If you wanted to give the middle class a $12,000 raise, just reduce regulations. Trust me, a $12,000 raise is a lot of money for middle class folks like you and I. As an example of the inefficiency, the DOE is working to revise energy regulation for HID lighting (those big old street lights that hum). However, innovation in LED lighting by the private sector will make them obsolete before the new standard takes effect. (You may have seen all the new LED lighting in your local store.)

An incredible amount of capital is destroyed due to the length of time required to get a payback on the cost of the regulation, and the fact that we never actually use appliances long enough to get a payback. Many times, the technology expires, or people replace that appliance before the payback is realized. So the regulatory approach is wasteful and likely never achieves the expected results. You never see the waste, because the costs are embedded into the products and you are none the wiser. Innovation and invention will save far more energy than reduction and compliance. That is why energy use reduction measurements show more impact from innovation and less impact from the regulatory programs. The free market is better at providing solutions, because the American spirit to compete, succeed and thrive drives us to invent better solutions. I understand that it is a difficult thing to get comfortable with, because there is no central control system. But if you believe in God, you understand that God is ultimately in control, and we aren't at liberty to change His plan. We can only change our part in His plan. What we should be working on are incentives to innovate in a host of areas, without preference to technology or purpose.

The government did not provide any incentives for the new LED lighting (until after it was commercialized), yet it exists today. In any case, you can see that the regulatory approach did not provide a meaningful reduction in energy use when compared to industry innovation. The LED light invented by industry in a free market will reduce lighting energy use by 85%.[21] Did you catch that? The new innovative lighting will reduce lighting energy use by 85%. The regulatory standards-driven programs all pale in comparison.

The Insitute for Energy Research did a study on regulation and energy costs in each state.[22] The more regulation and central control, the higher the energy costs. Higher energy costs lead to higher energy prices. I took the data from 48 states and graphed unemployment as a function of energy prices. The result is a full 2% higher unemployment rate overall in states with higher energy prices. Two percentage points is about 2.2 million workers and families. If those unemployed folks were earning just the median wage of $40,000 per year, their employment would create an additional $88.6 billion in wealth for middle class Americans. Those wages create an additional $12 billion in funding to social security and Medicare programs. Lower energy costs lead to lower unemployment and increased prosperity for the American people. Conversly, higher energy costs lead to higher unemployment and increased poverty.

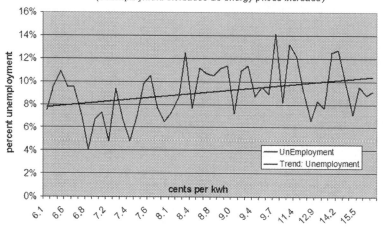

Unemployment as a Function of Energy Prices
(Unemployment increases as energy prices increase)

Source: Institute for Energy Research, 'Energy Regulation in the States: A Wake-up Call", http://www.instituteforenergyresearch.org/states/

Figure 17 Unemployment as a Function of Energy Prices (IER)

Summary

Equal access to our natural resources under the law is best accomplished when there are no preferential subsidies to oil or renewable energy, and limited additional taxes on business. Economic prosperity is best accomplished when regulations are few and the decisions about people, capital, and energy are made each day by people like you and I. In particular, taxes on energy reduce economic activity and produce energy poverty for the middle class. Subsidies and taxes ought to be replaced with relaxed regulations and an expedited process for areas where we want to encourage growth. Encourage growth by inserting more freedom. Equal protection under the law requires an end to preferential government-private partnerships. In the end, big government equals big abuse, small government equals far less abuse.

It is the measured risk and diversity of the free market that encourages innovation and the drive of the American entrepreneur.

The drive of the entrepreneur will produce the wealth of ideas which will solve our energy supply crisis.

On the other hand, it's the strangulation hold of central regulation and the subsequent confusion created in its wake that will prevent us from producing low-cost, clean and abundant energy to fuel our economy.

References

1   Congressional Research Service, R41227, "Energy Tax Policy: Historical Perspectives on and Current Status of Energy Tax Expenditures", Molly F. Sherlock Analyst in Economics, May 2, 2011

2   Congressional Budget Office, R43040, "How much does the Federal Government Support the Development and Production of Fuels and Energy Technologies", Terry Dinan and Philip Webre, March 6, 2012.

3   Caroline May, The Daily Caller, Federal Government Spent Nearly $70 billion on 'Climate change activities' since 2008, 5/17/2012 & Sen. James Inhofe CRS Report R14227 to Senate.

4   CRS, Congressional Research Service, "Energy Tax Policy: Historical Perspectives on and Current Status of Energy Tax Expenditures", R41227, May 2, 2011

5   Thiessen, Marc. Forget Bain, Obamas Public Equity Record is the Real Scandal, Washington Post Online, May 24, 2012, http://www.washingtonpost.com/opinions/forget-bain-obamas-public-equity-record-is-the-real-scandal/2012/05/24/gJQAXnXCnU_story.html

6   Annual Report FORM 20-F, filed June 30, 2011, Nevada Geothermal Power Inc.

7   US Dept of the Treasury Website, ARRA Section 1603 Program, June 12, 2012, http://www.treasury.gov/initiatives/recovery/Pages/1603.aspx

8   EIA, Office of Energy Statistics Report,"Performance Profiles of Major Energy Producers 2009", Feb 2011, http://www.eia.gov/finance/performanceprofiles/pdf/020609.pdf

9   EIA, Energy Information Administration, "Energy Explained", May 2012, http://www.eia.gov/energyexplained/

10 Anne Vandermey, "Flight Patterns", Fortune Magazine, Mar 21, 2011, p31.

11 API, American Petroleum Institute, "Putting Earnings Into Perspective", Jan 31, 2012, www.api.org/aboutoilgas

12 Bureau of Land Management, Oil and Gas Statistics, http://www.blm. gov/wo/st/en/prog/energy/oil_and_gas/statistics.html

13 Bureau of Land Management, http://www.blm.gov/

14 Institute for Energy Research, "Private and State Lands Producing 5.5 Times More Oil Per Acre", May 17, 2012, http://www.instituteforenergyresearch.org/2012/05/17/ private-and-state-lands-producing-5-5-more-oil-per-acre/

15 CBO, Congressional Budget Office, "Cost Estimate of H.R. 2454 American Clean Energy and Security Act of 2009", June 5, 2009, http:// www.cbo.gov/sites/default/files/cbofiles/ftpdocs/102xx/doc10262/ hr2454.pdf

16 Corey Boles, Martin Vaughan, "White House Official Boosts Cap and Trade Revenue Estimate", Wall Street Journal Online, March 17, 2009, http://online.wsj.com/article/SB123733423766063691.html

17 Review and Outlook, "Cap and Tax Fiction: Democrats off-loading economics to pass climate change bill.", Wall Street Journal Online, June 26, 2009, http://online.wsj.com/article/SB124588837560750781.html

18 Stephen Meyers, Alison Williams and Peter Chan, "Energy and Economic Impacts of U.S. Federal Energy and Water Conservation Standards Adopted From 1987 Through 2011", April 2012, http://ees.ead.lbl.gov/ bibliography/

19 Homepage of the Government site to list new regulations, www. regulations.gov, August 14, 2012

20 US Senator James M. Inhofe, "2011 Annual Report", December, 2011

21 DOE, Building Technologies Program, "Lifecycle Assessment of Energy and Environmental Impacts of LED Lighting Products, August 2012, http://apps1.eere.energy.gov/buildings/publications/pdfs/ ssl/2012_LED_Lifecycle_Report.pdf

22 Institute for Energy Research, *Energy Regulation in the States: A Wake-up Call*", Mar 27, 2013, http://www.instituteforenergyresearch.org/states/

CHAPTER 5

Air Pollution

The original goals the EPA set to control air pollution have been met. In 1970, there was acid rain in parts of the Midwest. Pollution was a real problem. Trash was an issue. Everyone wants clean water and parks. Many of the things that have been done in the last 40 years to clean up our environment have proven successful. However, it is difficult today to have a discussion about air pollution and energy generation because most people think that power plants destroy the environment. The perception that you must choose between clean air or electricity is a stubborn one.

A NREL (National Renewable Energy Laboratory) Study[1] asked the following question: *"Some people say that the progress of this nation depends on an adequate supply of energy and that we have to have it even though it means taking some risks with the environment. Others say the important thing is the environment, and that it is better to risk not having enough energy than to rick spoiling our environment. Are you more on the side of adequate energy or more on the side of protecting the environment?"* It's a red herring question. Given the improvement in generation efficiency and reduction in air emissions, we don't really have to choose one or the other. We have made tremendous progress in developing clean generation. Our achievements are simply wonderful. The power generation industry stepped up, met, and exceeded the air pollution goals set by the EPA. Now it's time to find an equilibrium between regulating pollution and encouraging innovation for low cost and plentiful energy sources.

We have turned the environmental clock backwards in the power generation industry. Further reductions and continued regulation are becoming ineffective due to the law of diminishing returns. Now we need to begin innovating our way out to the next level of improvement.

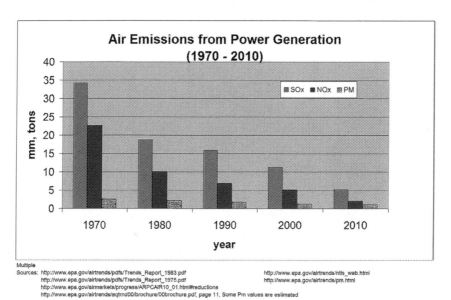

Multiple
Sources: http://www.epa.gov/airtrends/pdfs/Trends_Report_1983.pdf   http://www.epa.gov/airtrends/ntis_web.html
http://www.epa.gov/airtrends/pdfs/Trends_Report_1975.pdf   http://www.epa.gov/airtrends/pm.html
http://www.epa.gov/airmarkets/progress/ARPCAIR10_01.html#reductions
http://www.epa.gov/airtrends/aqtrnd00/brochure/00brochure.pdf, page 11, Some Pm values are estimated

Figure 18 Air Emissions from Power Generation (EPA)

Look at the Air Pollution From Power Generation chart and marvel at the reduction. (It sounds really cheesy to say it that way, but it really is an incredible result.) Breathe the air and feel the results. The SOx and NOx emissions have been reduced by 81% and 65% respectively by the EPA's own numbers.[2] The environmental folks feel the same way (sarcasm) because they have given up asking for reductions in whole numbers on top of reductions. The reduction charts would start to look silly if we use them to demand further reductions. If we were to cut current power generation SOx emissions in half it would only be a 10% reduction of the total since 1970. The remaining 10% reduces the emissions to zero. Therefore, what they will advertise in the media is their request for the 50% reduction of *current* emissions by 2020, for example. They leave out the detail that clarifies that it's a 10% reduction in overall emissions, because the numbers are so very small that the request would put us well past 90% of the way towards zero since 1970.

Air pollution overall has been reduced by over 68% since 1970[3], and we have delivered a rejuvenated environment. That turns the environmental clock backward and utilizes the measures and controls developed over 40 years to manage pollution. Air pollution overall has been reduced while vehicles, electricity and industry, and the economy have all increased at the same time. For all practical purposes, the EPA's goal has indeed been achieved.

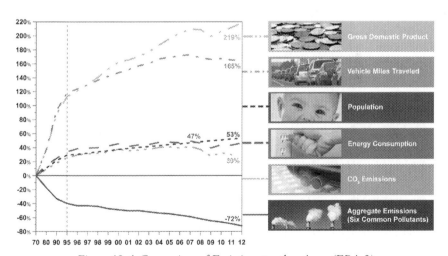

Figure 19 A Comparison of Emissions to other Areas (EPA-2)

The Uncertainty of Global Warming

I am not going to discuss the technical merits of the global warming issue. The earth was warm, then it cooled some, now it may be warmer. Rather, I want to introduce a new perspective and look at the whole issue through the filter of the previous chapters. Why is there actually a debate? At the highest level, I don't really care that some folks think that the earth is warming. I don't care that some folks think it is not warming. The issue becomes two-sided, because the big environmental group seeks to utilize the issue to assume a role of power over other people through government regulation. What I would like to point out is how bad of an idea regulations would be due to the complexity of the issue. The complexity introduces tremendous uncertainty. The impact of the uncertainty is amplified by the fact that there are alternate opinions both in the cause of global warming and the proposed solutions. The alternate opinions, and actual errors in the supporting data, are suppressed. No intellectually honest professional can review the data and consider the issue settled. Even if you did consider the issue settled and thought the climate was warming, the impact of that conclusion must still be considered within the backdrop of faith in order to respect religious freedoms.

We will simply use the analogy discussed earlier to highlight the issue. If we were trying to determine the answer to "what is 2+2", then the answer is simple. If you are trying to determine the best chocolate cake recipe, then the answer is more complex. The climate is exponentially more complex than a chocolate cake, as there is the atmosphere, cryosphere (glaciers), lithosphere (land), and ocean. All these systems are incredibly complex, and made even more complex by the fact that they all work together and feed energy back and forth, as a part of our biosphere. Then, it gets more complex when we consider that the earth is impacted tremendously by the sun. We don't even need a scientist to show us the impact of the sun on our climate. Step outside in January versus August in Michigan for 10 minutes. You will be come acutely aware that it is the sun that heats the earth. Then, the sun and the earth are all in our galaxy hurdling through space. Yes, our galaxy is actually moving through different parts of space as the universe expands. Some parts of our space are warmer than others. If there were just 3 main factors in each of the 6 major systems above, then there are 18 variables. If there is just 5% uncertainty in each variable, and the systems are first order (which means they multiply only once), then the mathematical uncertainty is additive, and the error in that calculation is 5% times 18 or 90% uncertainty. That means that in the given example, that there could be a 10% chance of being correct. The earth, atmosphere and space are infinitely complex.

A review of the accuracy of weather forecasting further highlights the unpredictability. In a short study of the numbers, from the book *Freakonomics* by Stephen J. Dubner,[4] we can see that the uncertainty in a 7-day weather forecast in their work was 7.5 degrees. That means that weather forecasts are off by an average of 7.5 degrees when only trying to forecast 7 days out. The big environment group is trying to predict a 0.4 degree change over 20 years. It's not likely that it can be done.

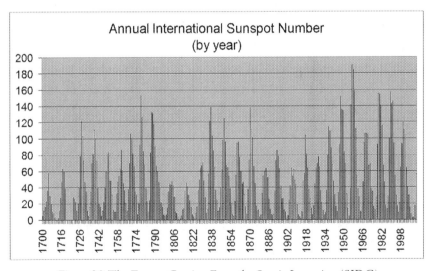

Figure 20 The Energy Coming From the Sun is Increasing (SIDC)

Add to the complexity the fact that scientists have different opinions, and the uncertainty clouding the issue grows. It is ok to have discourse, but it is not ok to make policy on the issue while there is so much disagreement. Many scientists and researchers dating back to the 1800s believe that the sun has the biggest impact on our climate.[5] Some researchers think the sun plays a larger role than presently accounted for in most climate models. The climate models seem to all focus on the man-made impacts, not nature. The Intergovernmental Panel on Climate Change (IPCC) notes in their latest report[6] that there are 8 different man-made factors they use to model the earth's climate, among them carbon. There is only one natural factor, the sun. Even more interesting is that when they use these components, they have to assign to them a "weight" or an importance. This should be done through observation, testing and research. They call this "weighting" a radiative forcing measure. It is a measure of the influence that a factor has in affecting the climate in the earth-atmosphere system. It is an index of the importance of the factor as a potential cause of climate change. The IPCC assumes carbon is 14 times more dominant in the climate than is the sun. They make these choices based on their opinion as opposed to letting the empirical data drive the model. I recently read a study that showed a very strong correlation of .85 between the sun and earth air temperatures between 1600 and today. This study further noted that the Intergovernmental Panel on Climate Change (IPCC) used too low of a radiative forcing for the power of the sun in the IPCC's second report, and that the sun is likely responsible for about half all global warming up to 1970. Many alternate opinions like these are thus far not included in the models.

Given that there are a wide range of opinions in this very complex issue, we would think that there would be some conflict oriented discussion. The alternate opinions are there, but you have to listen for them, because they play against the political media bias that there is a global warming consensus. In 2010, the IPCC had to retract some controversial statements in their 4th Assessement Report. Glaciologists pointed out that the statement concerning the Himalayan glaciers receding faster than in any other part of the world was wrong. This led to identifying other poorly sourced claims in the IPCC report according to an article in *The Economist*.[7]

The IPCC's 3rd Assessment Report included a now famous chart which showed that temperatures were rising, almost shooting higher, indicating incontrovertable global warming. Al Gore used that chart, which is now referred to as the "hockeystick" chart because the temperatures were flat (strangely even through the Medieval ice age), then shot upwards like the end of a hockey stick. However, other researchers questioned the report and then discredited it. Then the US Congress got involved and commissioned the National Research Council to investigate. They found some minor errors, but then they themselves were investigated. So there were found statistical errors in the original report, as well as in others' reports of the report, all relating back to the original "hockeystick" chart that showed intense global warming in 2010.[8] There is no concensus. It has been 15 years since Al Gore gave us the message that we only have 10 years left and the earth will melt away, or some such silly dire, end-of-the-world warning. The predictions have been proved false by time. So how is that we have all these models showing global warming? It is because everyone is looking for it. If you have ever looked for shapes in the clouds, you know that you will find them—which is equivalent to bad science of the first order.

I'll leave you with two last thoughts to consider on the uncertainty of the global warming issue. In 1965, there was a project called Bios 3 that was supposed to recreate a stable ecosystem. Then later, in 1991 we started the Biosphere 2 program. Remember the big biosphere dome that was supposed to be a human-designed replica of nature, a self-sustaining environment? People were going to be locked inside and show that we could live a self-sustained life. Well both of those projects were unsuccessful at creating a prolonged balanced environment. The lesson is that we don't even have enough understanding to create just one small ecosphere and make it work, yet somehow we are supposed to believe that scientists are going to predict a .4 degree temperature rise over 20 years on this giant biosphere called earth? I don't believe it. Lastly, there is an old analogy called the watchmakers' challenge[9] which argues that something that is obviously of intricate design, must have a designer. It goes like this:

In crossing a heath, suppose I pitched my foot against a stone, and were asked how the stone came to be there; I might possibly answer, that, for anything I knew to the contrary, it had lain there forever: nor would it perhaps be very easy to show the absurdity of this answer. But suppose I had found a watch upon the ground, and it should be inquired how the watch happened to be in that place; I should hardly think of the answer I had before given, that for anything I knew, the watch might have always been there. (…) There must have existed, at some time, and at some place or other, an artificer or artificers, who formed [the watch] for the purpose which we find it actually to answer; who comprehended its construction, and designed its use. (…) Every indication of contrivance, every manifestation of design, which existed in the watch, exists in the works of nature; with the difference, on the side of nature, of being greater or more, and that in a degree which exceeds all computation.

The point is that the ecosystem is very complex (like the watch analogy) and has many intricacies and complexities. Things that are complex, by all logical conjecture, have an obvious purpose for which they are designed. They also have a designer. Therefore, due to the complexity and obvious design, our ecosystem has a designer. Our being here is a part of the design, not a flaw in the design.

Old Generation

We have been building coal generation plants for many years. We have generation stations operating today that were put into service in the 1950s. We did not even have color television in the 1950s. In addition, the TVs of that time still had to have the channel changed by walking up to the TV and turning an actual knob. (I mean really, can you imagine the inconvenience). The first widespread use of color television broadcast did not happen until 1965. The fact that we can keep these old coal plants running and profitable is on one hand a testament to American ingenuity and the skill of the American worker. It is at the same time a testament to the failure of government regulation.

Meanwhile, there are 564 coal plants that were put into service prior to 1978.[10] Those plants are responsible for 60% to 70% of all SOx/NOx air emissions and about 45% of our electricity generation. The old TVs were made obsolete by new technology and improved to the point whereby the economics did not make sense to keep the old black and white TVs around. Today, people are getting rid of their old color TVs by their own choice in favor of new flat screen high definition TVs that connect to the Internet. At the same time, regulations have preserved the venerable old power plants by eliminating the choice of easy and economical replacement. The result is bad for our economy and bad for the environment. The old generating stations emit more pollution. The electric generation industry has improved tremendously. There has been an overall 93% reduction in emissions from power generation plants started up, or "re-powered," after 2000. It is only regulation and the big environment group that stops us from replacing these older, high pollution, less efficient generation stations.

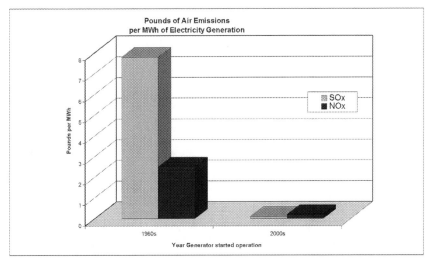

Figure 21 Air Emissions from Old Generation –vs– New (NETL)

Summary

The emissions reduction and cleanup of the environment from 1970 to today has been a great success. We are almost 70% of the way to zero emissions. At this point we have to question where the equilibrium point lies. What comes next? If it is the environmentalists' goal to achieve zero emissions on power generation, then they should also understand what is being given up in the economy in return for zero emissions. The fact is we will not be able to reduce our energy use to zero. What is needed is a bridging plan to move us economically beyond the current technological challenges to a new era of energy sources. How were our jet airliners, our cars, our TVs and our appliances powered 100 years ago? The answer? We did not have most of those technological advances 100 years ago. The answer to the energy question is the same, in that we will likely not be talking about coal and natural gas 100 years from now. Therefore, it is not wise or strategic to base so much permanent pollution law and regulation on today's energy sources.

The EPA was founded with the idea that economic development of any nature should not proceed without a due diligence step to ascertain the environmental impact. The reverse should also be true for economic impact. Since the founding of the EPA, the goals and measures have been refined and reduced to continue a march towards zero air pollution. Our economic health is just as important as our ecology. Green space and pristine, zero-energy buildings are of no use to the unemployed father trying to feed his family. Just as we looked forward in 1970 to set a course for the environment, we should also take a look forward today and ask ourselves what our priorities are for energy in the next century. We should also ascertain the economic impact and set some economic goals for the years ahead. Those goals should include economic due process for any future environmental controls.

Finally, keep in mind that the potential for error is high, the actual consensus on global warming is low—and the impact on the economy is high. Pollution and the global warming topic is not an issue upon which to base lasting legislation.

References

1   NREL, National Renewable Energy Laboratory, "Trends in Public
    Perceptions and Preferences on Energy and Environmental Policy",
    NREL/TP-461-4857a, March 1993

2   EPA, 2013, National Emissions Inventory (NEI) Air Pollutant Emissions
    Trends Data, http://www.epa.gov/ttn/chief/trends/ , 1970 - 2012 Average
    annual emissions, all criteria pollutants in MS Excel - June 2013.

3   EPA, Air Quality Trends, http://www.epa.gov/airtrends/images/
    comparison70.jpg

4   Stephen J. Dubner, "How Valid Are T.V. Weather Forecasts?",
    Freakonomics, http://www.freakonomics.com/2008/04/21/
    how-valid-are-tv-weather-forecasts/

5   Peter N. Spotts, "Are sunspots prime suspects in global warming?", The
    Christian Science Monitor, September 27, 2007, http://www.csmonitor.
    com/2007/0927/p13s03-sten.html

6   IPCC, 2007: Summary for Policymakers. In: Climate Change 2007:
    The Physical Science Basis. Contribution of Working Group I to the
    Fourth Assessment Report of the Intergovernmental Panel on Climate
    Change [Solomon, S., D. Qin, M. Manning, Z. Chen, M. Marquis, K.B.
    Averyt, M.Tignor and H.L. Miller (eds.)]. Cambridge University Press,
    Cambridge, United Kingdom and New York, NY, USA.

7   Briefing The science of climate change, "the clouds of unknowing", The
    Economist, March 20th, 2010, p83

8   Wikipedia contributors, 'Hockey stick controversy', Wikipedia, The
    Free Encyclopedia, 25 August 2012, http://en.wikipedia.org/w/index.
    php?title=Hockey_stick_controversy&oldid=509069678

9   Wikipedia contributors, 'Watchmaker analogy', Wikipedia, The Free Encyclopedia, 12 August 2012, http://en.wikipedia.org/w/index.php?title=Watchmaker_analogy&oldid=507091097

10 GAO, Government Accountability Office, "Air Emissions and Electricity Generation at U.S. Power Plants", Apr 2012, GAO-12-545R

CHAPTER 6

Efficient, Economical and Clean, Energy

Energy Use and Efficiency

The lowest cost energy is to find a way to use less; it is energy efficiency. The cost to reduce energy use is about 30% of the cost to generate energy. However, energy efficiency has boundaries. We will not be able to reduce our way to energy prosperity. How much energy do we use each year? Usage per person has remained largely level and has even dropped slightly over the last 35 years.[1] As a nation of people, we are more efficient (see figure: Energy Use and Efficiency). However, the population has increased, so overall use has increased along with the population. The most dramatic result is that energy use per dollar of manufactured product has decreased sharply.[2] Businesses and manufacturers have become dramatically more efficient. Energy use compared to gross domestic product has decreased by about 55% from 17 thousand BTUs to about 7 thousand BTUs per dollar. Notice that the reduction in energy use for business and manufacturing was taking place prior to the creation of the EPA, at about the same rate right through the first energy supply crisis created under President Carter. There is no change in the rate of reduction. When we look

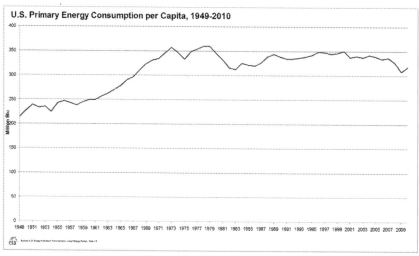

Figure 22 Energy Use is Steady Per Person (EIA)

closer at the amount of energy saved, as tracked by government programs, we see that the Energy Star Program saved 240 billion kilowatt-hours[3] of energy, or about 2% of our total use reduction over 35 years of impact. This comes from the Energy Star annual reports. But our total energy use compared to gross domestic product has dropped by 55% or more when you look at Figure 17. So we see that business and manufacturing folks not reporting or aligned with the program actually saved an incredible amount of energy. America as a whole saved 25 times the energy that was accounted for in the government programs. Certainly there are other coordinated impacts with the Energy Star program, but they cannot account for a 25 times reduction. This supports the conculsion that we were reducing energy use at about the same rate prior to the creation of the EPA. Businesses implement energy efficiency measures because they just make good business sense. Looking at the result, we see regulation produced a 2% reduction in use, whereby individual, free market effort produced a

53% reduction in use. The solutions are best applied and results greatly magnified when people are free to implement ideas on thier own.

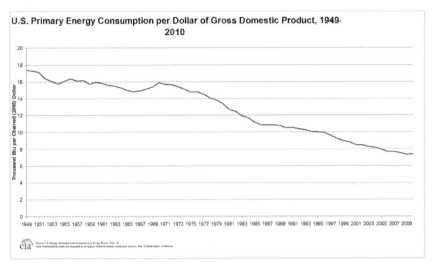

U.S. Primary Energy Consumption per Dollar of Gross Domestic Product, 1949-2010

Figure 23 Energy Use Drops Sharply Compared to Manufacturing Output (EIA)

Now, don't interpret the example to mean that the Energy Star program is not effective. The Energy Star program is a great application towards the solution because it helps to educate people about energy use, provides a technical resource, and is voluntary, so it leaves people free to implement solutions based on their own views. It is a good expression of the Constitutional role of the Federal Government to "promote the general welfare." The Energy Star Program does not exclude other market programs from working. On the contrary, it provides a method of comparing the many different efficiency solutions developed by a free market. However, energy efficiency (while a great low-cost option) cannot get us all the way to a prosperous energy supply strategy. We also need more generation. We are using more energy today due to our higher population, not due to business or industrial waste, misuse, or lack of regulation.

Price is an important component of free market, clean energy solutions. Let's look at energy prices and how they impact supply and demand versus regulatory controls' impact on supply and demand.

Transportation energy use has decreased over the last 40 years. That use reduction aligns with the 1970s timeframe and the increased focus on the energy issue. The first National Energy Policy was adopted in about 1975 as a part of Project Independence. Project Independence was intended to stabilize auto fuel prices. You can look at the results and see the stability proposed by government control never happened. Government involvement (neither democrat nor republican) has helped to stabilize gasoline prices for us in the last 40 years. In fact, you can look at the result over the last 70 years and see that a centrally controlled energy policy is quite clearly aligned with the problem. Secondly, industrial energy costs decreased up to the 1970s, and then increased. As costs increased, use decreased. Energy use decreased most in the sector with the most sensitivity to cost— our business and industrial energy prices. Additionally, when we plot usage against costs for industrial energy use, we see that even after the government programs were in place and were well-established, energy use increased for a period in the 1980s when electricity prices decreased. The correlation of energy use to price is solid. There are at least 4 instances on the chart that show the direct correlation of use to price changes. During this period, all the government programs were still in full swing. The fact that there are government programs does not impact energy use even remotely as much as price impacts energy use. These elements show that the marketplace and price signals are a much stronger driver of use and behavior than a national energy policy. There is a quotation from Milton Friedman, that applies here:

"Nobody spends somebody else's money as carefully as he spends his own. Nobody uses somebody else's resources as carefully as he uses his own. So if you want efficiency and effectiveness, if you want knowledge to be properly utilized, you have to do it through the means of private property."

—Milton Friedman (1912 - 2006)
American Nobel Laureate economist

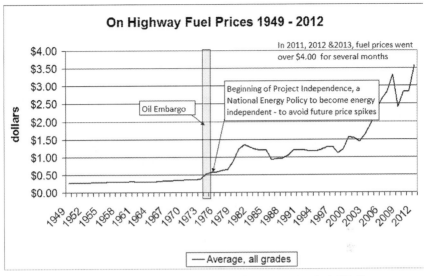

Figure 24 A National Energy Policy has Never Worked (EIA)

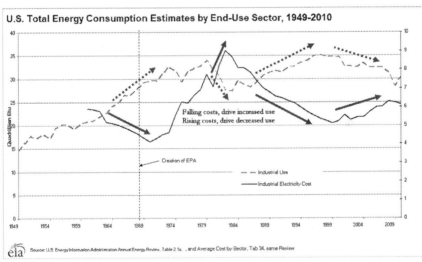

Figure 25 The Market Drives Energy Use Reductions (EIA)

The big environmental groups would do much better by advocating and promoting general efficiency than they would by focusing people on a singular energy solution, and controlling and regulating towards one solution. While certain programs do well to promote a useful impact and educate people, the government taking credit for the tremendous efficiency in our economy is, well, unfounded.

Clean Energy Generation

What is clean energy? For the purposes of this discussion, clean energy is different from green energy. Green energy represents the class of energy that the environmentalist movement supports. It's hard to have a measured goal of green energy because environmentalist groups seem to choose their favorite energy with differing criteria, and it's an all or none proposition. The environmentalist is against potential spills of chemicals at gas drilling and fracturing sites. Fracturing compounds are typically 90% water, 9% sand and about 1% salts, glycols, and alcohols. However, the environmentalist is ok with the potential for chemical spills in silicon film deposition processes for solar panels, which use arsine and phosphine, cadmium and lead. What happens to those materials when the PV panel is retired after 20 years? Also consider that capturing and pumping carbon (CO_2) into the ground poses as much of a risk as any other gas. The CO_2 they want to pump into the ground is a gas and can escape just like any other gas, such as ammonia, which is also used to test PV panels. If the CO_2 escapes, it is heavier than air and it could be a suffocation danger to people living in the vicinity of the CO_2 storage facility. So, for this discussion, clean energy is a direct comparison of the actual emission result of the power production process. Clean energy is also a measurable goal. It is not all or none. We should be willing to support *cleaner* energy on our way to *clean* energy.

The new 2010 era coal power plants are 93% cleaner overall than the old 1960s era power plants. The new 2010 era power plants are only 7% away from being as clean as renewable energy. The NOx emissions are 99% less in new power plants than those operating prior to 1970. The SOx emissions are 92% lower in new power plants than compared to those operating prior to 1970. We could, as a nation, reduce our emissions due to electricity generation by over 95%, just by replacing old coal technology with new coal technology. The new coal plants are 20% to 40%

more electrically efficient as well, creating economic efficiency and therefore creating economic activity. Take a look at the charts and see the gains in efficiency and in clean technology that have already been achieved by the power generation industry. It is easy to see now how the current argument by the big environment lobby distracts us by keeping us focused on the wrong issues. The environmental lobby's focus is on the two new generation types (right side of Figure 25) as opposed to the 1960s era coal plants. So the current argument today is between selecting the technology that is 93% (new coal and gas) better or 99% better (renewables and carbon capture). The big environment group is at a stalemate with the big oil group over the last 7% of emissions. It is paralysis by analysis. Meanwhile, those old coal plants represent about 45% of our electricity generation. If we choose to segment a smaller group, about 30% of emissions and 20% of our electrical power is generated with the 1960s era coal plants. Those are the coal plants built prior to the invention of color television. Most of our pollution emissions come from the very old power plants, not power plants in general.

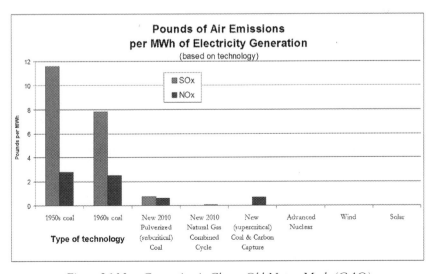

Figure 26 New Generation is Clean, Old Not so Much (GAO)

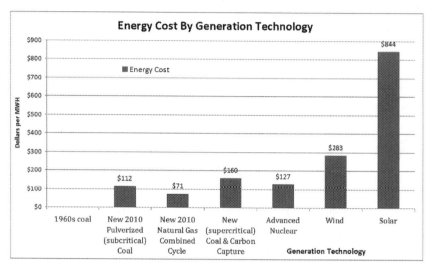

Figure 27 Renewable Energy (as a Replacement Technology) is Expensive (NETL)

The second piece of data you need to look at is the increased cost of the renewable technologies on the right side of the cost figure (figure 26). They are clearly two ($160) to ten times ($844) more expensive.[4] One reason they are so expensive is because we need to install so much more capital if they are to be a replacement technology. Solar energy is only available 25% of the time. Therefore, four (4) times as many solar panels need to be installed to provide storage and have energy available all the time. That cost does not take into account transmission needs, so it is likely a little low.

In the end, it is the distraction regarding the last 7% of air emissions that keeps the big energy industry from replacing the old generation with new, cleaner energy generation using low cost domestic fuel. The environmental and regulatory folks should be thinking, "We have met the enemy, and it is us". If we follow the big environment plan and replace the current 1960s and older generation with baseload renewable energy or carbon sequestration that costs more and produces less energy, then we will destroy economic value and reduce economic activity. It will be taxing on the middle class. A better option is to replace all the old 1960s era generation with new 2010 era coal and gas generation as an interim measure. We can increase efficiency and economic activity and reduce emissions of the old generating stations at the same time. It should be clear to any person looking at the data that this is a great compromise. Replacing the 1960s era generation would reduce remaining air emissions by over 30%, which is a tremendous amount. If we replaced all the generation prior to 1978 with new coal and natural gas generation then we would reduce the present emissions by up to 70%. That would take us from 93% of the way to zero emissions up to 97% of the way to zero emissions. Furthermore, we would do it with increased efficiency and create unimaginable economic activity. Incredible! The great drive in the human spirit to innovate, explore and achieve has produced nothing short of incredible new technology in the energy generation industry. Let's use it.

If we were to replace the 1960s coal generation stations with current 2010 era coal and gas generation stations, it will take us 20 years. We could commit to replacing the 400 worst generation stations in the next 20 years. In the same timeframe, we should work to develop more cost effective conventional generation, nuclear fission, nuclear fusion and renewable energy technology. Yes, I am advocating a true all of the above approach which includes renewable energy. Renewable energy will not likely produce lower cost energy (as a *replacement* technology) in the next 50 years. Look at how long it has taken to be 4 to 10 times more expensive than fossil fuel. Evenso, we do not want to limit our choices before the research work is done. Renewable energy when used as a *supplemental* technology may certainly have an effective place in generation strategies. Let's allow technology and the free market to make those choices. The good ideas will spread, the bad ones won't.

So while the environmentalist is trying to spend even more money to pump CO^2 down into the ground (nevermind that we don't know those environmental and health impacts), multiple improvements to the Oxy-fuel cycle have developed. The Oxy fuel cycle functions by observing that the air pumped into a coal fired electric generator is only 21% oxygen and the rest is a gas mixture which ends up in the emissions. By purifying the air and feeding the combustion cycle with 100% oxygen the efficiency is improved and the emissions are reduced by 80%[5]. One company has gone a step further and uses the small amount of CO^2 gasses that are created to then enhance the recovery of oil from tight oil fields by pumping the CO^2 deep, deep into the ground (much deeper than sequester mines). Even without the treatment of the CO^2, this technology can provide great results because the NOx emissions are reduced by 80%. This puts the overall reduction of NOx from the 1970s era at about 98%. It sounds like a fabulous synergy of technology.

Another option for clean energy generation is nuclear energy. Nuclear and solar energy have both been around for 40+ years. Nuclear energy is very close to the cost of current generation technologies, while solar is not. A concerted effort to produce nuclear energy with a focus on safety and cost reduction would be a great goal.

The nuclear energy approach does have a big hurdle of where to store or reconstitute all the spent nuclear fuel. However, we put a man on the moon before we had any real computing power. We can solve this problem. France presently provides about 75% of their power through nuclear reactors and reconstitutes their fuel with minimal trouble. Environmentalists like to point to Europe when it is convenient, but why not take some hints from their use of nuclear power? Take into account that only about 20% of a nuclear fuel rod is "used up" in a nuclear reaction. Thus, we are throwing out about 80% of the good fuel due to lack of reconsituting technology. There are also other nuclear reactor designs, such as travelling wave reactors, which could use the 80% of the fuel that is left over. Some of those designs are said to be able to operate for 100 years on a single fueling event. Furthermore, these reactors utilize the wasted fuel rods from other reactors. That is even more fantastic. Another emerging idea is nuclear fission. Nuclear fission has been around as long as the sun. It is more efficient and has 90% less nuclear waste than fusion. Problem solved. I know it is not that simple, but we have to have some support for truly clean and economical energy generation.

It is likely that the fossil fuels will run out. But, it is our responsibility to produce, for our children, new replacement technologies at the same cost basis as we enjoyed. Just because something will happen is not a reason in and of itself to accelerate the outcome. By forcing us to abandon fossil fuels too early, we are driving costs up and wasting our capital and efforts on useless regulatory activities. The regulation of the power generation industry does not produce new and economical energy. That capital and those efforts could be applied to replace the older technology. There is an old adage from General Kutozov in *War and Peace*, that says "The strongest of all warriors are these two: Time and Patience". From this we get Kutuzovs maxim, "When in doubt, do nothing"[6]. Thus is the error of the big oil group and our congress in allowing the big environment group to rush forward, forcing us to abandon all our fossil fuel generation too early, in favor of solutions that are not yet economical nor technically viable. Instead, let's not concentrate our efforts on regulating and abandoning those fuels. Let's apply Kutuzov's maxim and wait. Let's allow time and patience for the marketplace of ideas come up with better, more economic replacements for our energy sources, turning our efforts to multiple ideas for replacement generation. Patience requires faith and trust in something outside of your own understanding. The future of big oil will prove to be self-determining. Most of the effort on regulating fossil fuels is wasted. The question for us is: What will replace big oil? The task for us is to make big oil obsolete through better economics and better ideas.

Fuel Supply

A *National Geographic* article[7] in 1981 claimed, "Nuclear energy, for example, already provides a tenth of the electricity in the United States, and would be capable of rapid expansion if licensing procedures were greatly sped up." Back in 1981 they thought the regulations were too constrictive, and today they have only gotten worse.

The message is simple. The truth is that today we have enough fossil fuel for hundreds and hundreds of years. It is likely also true that it will run out. It is a finite resource. The dichotomy of those ideas is the best reason to unleash the resources we have, and in the time remaining, apply our energy (pun intended) to inventing new generation technology beyond oil and gas, with all the innovation strength we have. To constrain our economy with extreme conservation does two things. First, it gives false hope that we can make this energy last forever. Second, it focuses us on conservation instead of innovation. The solution is several-fold. First, utilize better technology with less regulation to more inexpensively extract the resources we have in oil, gas and coal. Then, begin a more effective search for the next generation fuel using the funding resources that are re-focused away from regulation.

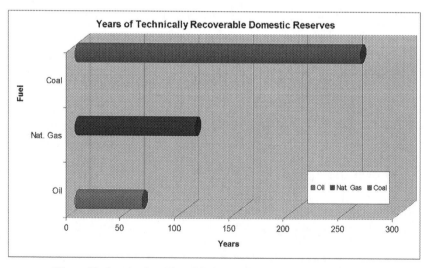

Figure 28 America has Plentiful Energy Resources (CRS: R40872)

We have more fossil fuel than Saudi Arabia. (Check the graphics on the following pages.) If we stopped paying high prices for foreign oil, we could also use that funding to innovate our way out of our energy supply crisis. The first step is to release US companies to mine, extract, ship and process the fuels we have. We have over 50 years of domestic oil supply, over 100 years of natural gas, and over 250 years worth of coal. That is just considering the resources that are known and technically recoverable. We have discovered more natural gas than we have used every year since the 1970s and there does not appear to be an end in sight yet. To be more clear, we thought there were only 50 years of technically recoverable oil in 1970 as well. This not to say that we have a license to waste energy over the next 100 years. Rather, it is even more important to find innovative, economical and clean energy sources, upon which to build our economy. That is a different goal than finding zero emission renewable energy sources, which cost more, and destroy economic value, while providing less service. Building the economy with energy means more energy output for less input. Building the economy with energy means energy is more plentiful. Innovation means turning the brilliant business and government minds of our time loose to solve the problem creatively. The government has been trying to solve the energy supply crisis through regulation since the 1970s and it has only gotten worse. The best years from an import persepective were in 1970 and prior years. In those years we imported about 23% of our oil and liquid fuels. Today, after 40 years of help from the Federal Government, we import 49% of our oil and liquid fuels. We're going backwards under the regulatory approach.

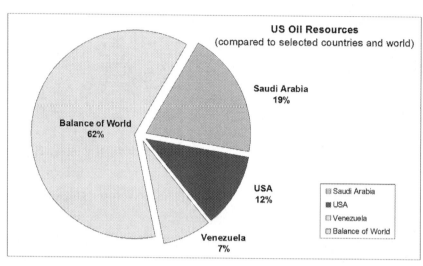

Figure 29 US Oil Resources, and the World (CRS: R40872)

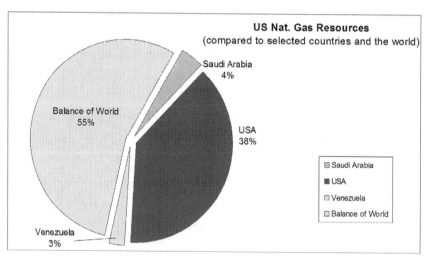

Figure 30 US Natural Gas Resources, and the World (CRS: R40872)

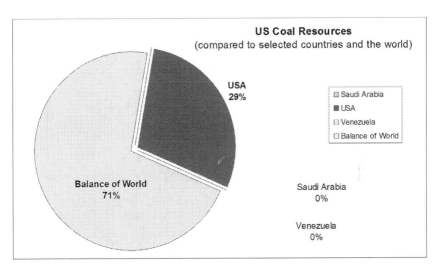

Figure 31 US Coal Resources, and the World (CRS: R40872)

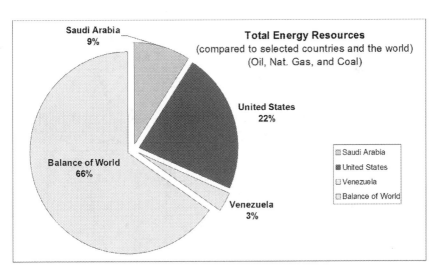

Figure 32 US Total Energy Resources, and the World (CRS: R40872)

As this book went to press, the updated Energy Information Administration's Annual Energy Outlook for 2013 was released.[8] It shows the tremendous growth of oil and natural gas resources given the shale discoveries in our own country. There is a 44% increase in US natural gas reserves and about a 100% increase in oil reserves, just in the last 2 years. We should note that the EIA is also very conservative in their numbers, which is why we appear to be finding more every year.

These numbers represent only the technically recoverable resources. The International Energy Outlook was not published in 2012 and is not yet available for 2013, so the charts above cannot be recalculated yet. However, it is very likely that the US now owns as much as 40% of the world's energy resources.

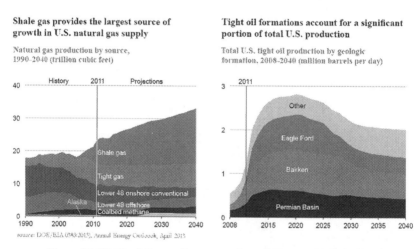

Figure 33 US Total Energy Resources, Annual Energy Outlook (EIA)

Summary

The challenge for us in discovering a clean, efficient and economical energy source is to determine the most useful and cost effective role for government to help promote a prosperous and clean energy industry. Price and energy efficiency are tied at the hip. People will reduce use when there is truly a benefit in it for them. The diverse and innovative approach of many people is more effective than a single or focused technology. Therefore, the most effective approach for a growing economy through energy prosperity, consists of only limited energy policy and a wealth of ideas and freedom.

We must consider a number of factors to create a prosperous energy economy. Here is a short list of required attributes for energy prosperity in our economy:

1. The rate of use must match the energy density. Namely, a 747 airliner will not function on solar panels. If there is not enough energy density to match the rate of use, we need to store energy for when we do need to use it. Coal, oil and nuclear fuel have a great amount of energy stored up in their mass.

2. The energy source must be efficient to store or transport. Wind and sunlight cannot be stored at all in their native form, they need to be processed at the rate they are collected. Electrical energy cannot be stored either, but it can be transported for about a 10% loss. Energy sources like coal, gasoline, natural gas and nuclear fuel are efficient to store.

3. Energy sources need to be able to be stored as a stable mass. Since the energy in coal, wood, or petroleum fuel is stored as stable mass, it is almost 100% efficient to store. It is a very convenient design. Coal and oil have a very high energy density, much higher than wood has stored in itself. However, gasoline, natural gas and nuclear fuel are not so stable to store.

4. The energy source and use must be matched in thier thermal or mechanical properties and uses. Water flowing over a wheel, or wind turning a wheel are great for grinding grain and pumping water. Coal and wood are great for burning and heating our homes and wash water. Electricity can turn an electric motor, such as in an EV car or industrial motor.

5. The fuel source must be efficient to process. We don't want to waste fuel, because it is limited, and because it makes energy more expensive. Fossil fuel generation is about 49% efficient. If we combine the heat and power for multiple uses, the efficiency is closer to 80%. Solar PV cells are about 21% efficient. However, solar cells and wind energy are working off renewable energy. The efficiency of renewable energy is most important in making it economical, and less about the resource since it is renewable. For example, a 20-year payback on PV solar generation that no longer functions after 20 years is not efficient or economical. Solar cells lose efficiency and eventually stop working.

6. Our energy sources should be clean. However, clean is only one of seven requirements, and cannot be the uber goal, trumping all other energy needs to get to 100% emissions-free generation. If we are honest, clean energy should also take into account the processing and retirement pollution from solar cells. Presently fossil fuel energy is 93% as clean as renewable energy, and I submit that there are many current generation technologies that meet this criteria, without the great expense of renewable energy.

7. Energy for our economy should be economical. Economical means it should be the same cost or less costly if possible when compared to todays energy costs. Any increase in costs is born unequally by the lower and middle class. Increased spending on energy has a direct impact on the economy, lowering the standard of living, because any additional income spent on energy comes directly out of the economy somewhere else and reduces economic activity. Conversly, lower energy costs release capital to be spent in other parts of the economy, lifting every person's standard of living.

The USA is blessed to be one of the most resource-rich nations on earth. While Saudi Arabia has a lot of oil, we have more natural gas than Saudi Arabia, and more coal than there is oil in all of the Middle East. We have a tremendous amount of coal, and coal, if you recall, is very energy dense. It is stable under transport, and is moved literally via open rail car. Today, when a coal mine is closed after production, it is remediated and planted with grass and topsoil. Those closed mines are beautiful prairies now. Coal is a great fuel. When you look at the total of all our fuel resources, it's obvious there is no reason that we should be an energy importer. How we develop our resources will determine our economy and the legacy we leave our children for the next century.

References

1   EIA, Energy Information Administration,"Annual Energy Review 2010", October 19, 2011, http://www.eia.gov/totalenergy/data/annual/perspectives.cfm

2   Ibid

3   EnergyStar and Other Climate Protection Partnerships, 2010 Annual Report, Figure 1.

4   NETL, National Energy Technology Laboratory, "Cost and Performance Baseline for Fossil Energy Plants Volume 1: Bituminous Coal and Natural Gas to Electricity", Nov 2010

5   NETL, National Energy Technology Laboratory, "Coal Fired Power Plants, Oxy Fuel Combustion", accessed June 2013, http://www.netl.doe.gov/technologies/coalpower/cfpp/technologies/oxy_combustion.html

6   Jonah Goldberg, "Dans le'doute, abstiens toi", National Review, Dec 31, 2009

7   Kenneth F. Weaver, "Our Energy Predicament", National Geographic, February, 1981, p19.

8   EIA, Energy Information Administration, "Annual Energy Outlook", April 2013, Figures 91,97

CHAPTER 7

We Power Us

L et's look at the guidance of our founding fathers. I have inserted
emphasis for those words that are no longer a common part of
our conversations. From Alexander Hamilton:

> *"The prosperity of commerce is now perceived and acknowledged by all
> enlightened statesmen to be the most useful as well as the most productive
> source of national wealth, and has accordingly become a primary object
> of their political cares. By multipying the means of gratification, by
> promoting the introduction and circulation of the precious metals [money],
> those darling objects of human avarice [desire for wealth] and enterprise,
> it serves to vivify [revive] and invigorate the channels of industry, and
> to make them flow with greater activity and copiousness [abundance].
> The assiduous [careful] merchant, the laborious husbandman, the active
> mechanic, and the industrious manufacturer,--all orders of men, look
> forward with eager expectation and growing alacrity [cheerful readiness]
> to this pleasing reward of their toils [work]"* (Alexander Hamilton,
> Federalist Papers #12, Tuesday, November 27, 1787).

There are currently two classes of people in America, the wealthy ruling class and the rest of us. What if the people who work and pay taxes were in charge instead of politicians? I think the following tasks need to be accomplished in order that we may pursue our individual goals and thereby achieve some measure of personal satisfaction and reward for our work. These several things would at once lift each person's standard of living, most noticeably in the lower and middle income classes. These actions would invigorate, in Alexander Hamilton's words, the economy through freedom in the energy industry. These changes would provide wealth and structural economic benefits to ourselves, and to our posterity. At the same time, these things are a big step towards achieving a large measure of results for the big environmental groups as well. If we implement the steps below, pollution would be reduced 30% to 70% and we would truly be searching for next generation fuels.

1. **Problem:** The EPA, BLM, and DOE agencies are granted authority to regulate and enforce rules in an area of the economy. However, authority is given prior to identification of the problem or the measures to cure the problem and insure success. This is counter to constitutional principles. All powers not given to the federal government in the Constitution are reserved to the people and the states. The reasons this is done is to prevent a runaway government. Furthermore these entities are driven by director-secretaries, and not a multiple person governing board. This abdication of responsibility by congress places an enormous amount of power in a single, unelected person's hands. It is easy for a single person to make a mistake or misjudgement.

   Solution: It is more wise to have multiple ideas leading a group with such vast and presently unchecked authority. Amend each entity to be driven by a board of 5 commissioners (similar to the FCC). Each newly elected US President may replace two in any 4-year term, and appoint which person serves as the chairperson. This provides a more fair representation of the people and further divides the power of the office.

2. **Problem:** The current subsidy policies corrupt big business and the marketplace.

   Solution: Eliminate all specific energy subsidies (fossil fuel, oil, renewable, smart meter, etc.). Manufacturing and typical treatments for the tax code should not be affected.

3. **Problem**: Regulations are strangling businesses and raising energy costs for the middle class. Furthermore, these regulations are instituted by unelected and unchecked regulatory agencies. The following legislation puts the power back into the hands of the people.

   Solution: Pass the "Reigns Act";

   Solution: Pass the "Energy Tax Prevention Act of 2011," S bill 482.

   a. Modify Section 330 (b)(1)(B) to add

      i. (a) Power generation pollutant limits shall be frozen to comply with current clean air capabilities. As such, an emissions limit shall be in force of 1.0 pound per MWH for NOx and 1.0 pound per MWH for SOx. Carbon is not a pollutant.

   b. Modify Section 330 (b)(4) to include

      i. Mercury and Air Toxics Rule (MACT)

      ii. Cross State Air Pollution Rule (CSAPR)

      iii. Regional GreenHouse Gas Initiatives (RGGI)

   c. Modify Section 330 (b)(2)(C) to state up to $1B in total.

4. **Problem**: Regulations are strangling our search for new energy and unfairly supporting big environment. The EPA mission and goals are not pursued with a balanced approach of people, planet, and profits. Our economic health is not duly considered under current environmental policy.

   Solution: Pass the "Reigns Act"

   Solution: Freeze EPA funding levels at the current level and over time they will revert back to the 2008 budget levels (as a percent of government spending), as the economy grows. This level should be sufficient to maintain a balanced environmental protection agency.

5. **Problem**: Too many of our electric generating stations are old, thereby producing more pollution and less electricity from our fossil fuels. Develop and pass a "Clean and Efficient Generation" Act or executive order to expedite permitting for current clean generation, powered by domestic fuel.

   Solution: Expedite permitting to replace at least 400 old power plants over the next 20 years. If a plant began operation prior to 1978, all permitting, including air permits, should be expedited for "clean generation" such that all permitting is completed within 12 months, for a new plant with similar or expanded capacity on the same site. This "CleanGen" initiative would promote power generation plants operating at 93% less emissions than the 1978 era generation. The process would align with the energy tax prevention act and encourage building generating stations operating at less than 1.0 pounds per mwh of SOx and less than 1.0 pounds per Mwh of NOx. This initiative would increase efficiency, lower costs and would reduce air pollution by up to 30% all at the same time.

6. **Problem**: Government is too big and wastes the labors of the people. This is especially true in areas where it is technically

difficult for the public to understand the truth without having a minimum level of technical ability.

Solution: Pass a Constitutional Amendment to fix government spending at 20% of GDP. The government has historically operated at 20% of GDP. This forces government to concentrate on governance in the areas intended by the Constitution.

7. **Problem**: The Dodd Frank Act chokes small energy supply contracting with onerous regulations, constricting private companies' abilities to purchase long term energy solutions

   Solution: Repeal the Dodd Frank Act

8. **Problem**: Government regulations are too long, convoluted and poorly constructed.

   Solution: Pass a Constitutional Amendment or a "Read the Bill Act" that states: The Federal Government shall make all proposed legislation available for download from the Internet, and available in every public library in an easy-to-access format, after public announcement, for a minimum of 10 days plus 1 day for every 10 pages (referenced materials by section included), prior to taking up a vote. (For example, a 180-page bill with 20 pages of referenced sections would be available for 30 days. A 2,000 page bill would be available for 300 days prior to being voted on).

9. **Problem**: The government, big business and the mainstream media are in collusion to keep people dependent upon the government. There are 25 Senators that have served for longer than 34 years, and the longest is 51 years. There is no reason to have a senator in power for 51 years. The professional politicians create a bad environment for energy innovation.

   Solution: Pass a Constitutional Amendment for term limits. We need to insure that there is an automatic way to change our government. Representatives can serve for 9 terms or 18 years and Senators can serve for 3 terms or 18 years.

Get Involved

- Call your congressmen and support the specific acts noted above
- Join the conversation on twitter at @wepowerusdotcom

Get the Book

www.WePowerUs.com

www.Amazon.com/

www.westbowpress.com/

REFERENCES FOR FIGURES

CRS, Congressional Research Service, "WorldCom: The Accounting Scandal", RS21253, August 29, 2002

New York Times, "Adding up the Governments Total Bailout Tab", July 24, 2011, http://www.nytimes.com/interactive/2009/02/04/business/20090205-bailout-totals-graphic.html

McGuire, Bill "Fed Loaned Banks Trillions in Bailout", Bloomberg Reports on ABC News, Nov 28, 2011

Recovery.Gov, US Government Website, http://www.Recovery.gov/transparency/fundingoverview/

Kneale, Klaus, Paolo Turchioe, "Layoff Tracker", Forbes Online, 4/1/2010, http://www.forbes.com/2008/11/17/layoff-tracker-unemployement-lead-cx_kk_1118tracker.html

Jacobe, Dennis, Gallup Economy, "In U.S., 54% Have Stock Market Investments, Lowest Since 1999", April 20, 2011 www.gallup.com/poll/147206/stock-market-investments-lowest-1999.aspx

Shapiro, Robert J., Pham Nam D., "Who Owns America's Oil and Natural Gas Companies", Sonecon LLC, Oct 2011

The Whitehouse, "Blueprint for a Secure Energy Future", www.Whitehouse.gov, March 2011

CRS, Congressional Research Service, "Energy Tax Policy: Historical Perspectives on and Current Status of Energy Tax Expenditures", R41227, May 2, 2011

May, Caroline, The Daily Caller, "Federal Government Spent Nearly $70 billion on 'Climate change activities' since 2008", 5/17/2012 & Sen. James Inhofe CRS Report R14227 to Senate.

Thiessen, Marc. "Forget Bain, Obamas Public Equity Record is the Real Scandal", Washington Post Online, May 24, 2012, http://www.washingtonpost.com/opinions/forget-bain-obamas-public-equity-record-is-the-real-scandal/2012/05/24/gJQAXnXCnU_story.html

API, American Petroleum Institute, "Putting Earnings Into Perspective", Jan 31, 2012, www.api.org/aboutoilgas

EIA, Energy Information Administration, "Energy Explained", May 2012, http://www.eia.gov/energyexplained/

Guidestar, (Organizations were located through Guidstar. Data was sourced from each entities website for the most current year available. http://takeaction.guidestar.org/

EIA, Energy Information Administration,"Annual Energy Review 2010", October 19, 2011, http://www.eia.gov/totalenergy/data/annual/perspectives.cfm

BLM, Bureau of Land Management, Oil and Gas Statistics, http://www.blm.gov/wo/st/en/prog/energy/oil_and_gas/statistics.html

SIDC-team, World Data Center for the Sunspot Index, Royal Observatory of Belgium, Monthly Report on the International Sunspot Number, online catalogue of the sunspot index: http://sidc.oma.be/sunspot-data/ *Annual sunspot number

NETL, National Energy Technology Laboratory, "Cost and Performance Baseline for Fossil Energy Plants Volume 1: Bituminous Coal and Natural Gas to Electricity", Nov 2010 and GAO-12-545R Air Emissions and Electricity Generation at U.S. Power Plants, Apr 2012

EPA, Environmental Protection Agency, Dept of Air and Radiation, http://www.epa.gov/airtrends/

EPA-2, Environmental Protection Agency, Dept of Air and Radiation, http://www.epa.gov/airtrends/aqtrends.html

CRS, Congressional Research Service, "U.S. Fossil Fuel Resources: Terminology, Reporting, and Summary", R40872, March 2011

USGS, United States Geological Survey, Energy Resources Program, http://energy.usgs.gov/

GAO, Government Accountability Office, "Air Emissions and Electricity Generation at U.S. Power Plants", GAO-12-545R, Apr 2012

NETL, National Energy Technology Laboratory, "Cost and Performance Baseline for Fossil Energy Plants Volume 1: Bituminous Coal and Natural Gas to Electricity", Nov 2010

IER, Institute for Energy Research, "Energy Regulation in the States: A Wake-up Call", http://www.instituteforenergyresearch.org/states/

AEO, Energy Information Administration, "Annual Energy Outlook", DOE/EIA 0383 (2013), April 2013, www.eia.gov